A history of Britain's Park and Ride stations

PARKWAY RAILWAY STATIONS

MARK CHATTERTON

GRESLEY BOOKS

Acknowledgments

I am grateful for the input of Neil Aventi, Tim Maddocks, John Stretton, Laurence Waters and John Webb who provided either photographs or information for this book.

Also a big thank you to the following people at these Train Operating Companies for their input:
Sarah Loak at Chiltern Railways
Leanne Barrie at East Midlands Railway
Lewis Brencher at Transport for Wales
John Carter at Great Western Railway
Patricia Kameni at Greater Anglia
Andrew McGill at West Midlands Trains
Nina Morgan at Govia Thameslink Railway
Greg Suligowski at Merseyrail

All photographs are by the author unless otherwise stated.

First published in Great Britain in 2021
by Gresley Books
an imprint of Mortons Books Ltd
Media Centre
Morton Way
Horncastle LN9 6JR
www.mortonsbooks.co.uk
Copyright © Gresley Books 2021

ISBN 978-1-911658-44-3
The right of Mark Chatterton to be identified as the author of this work has been asserted in accordance with the Copyright, Designs and Patents Act 1988.
Typeset by Jayne Clements (jayne@hinoki.co.uk), Hinoki Design and Typesetting.
Printed and bound in Great Britain.
10 9 8 7 6 5 4 3 2 1

Contents

PARKWAY RAILWAY STATIONS

Introduction

It's the summer of 1971 and I'm on holiday with my parents in the Bristol area. I'm a gangly 13-year-old, heavily into trains and train spotting. I've spent an enjoyable day spotting at Bristol Temple Meads station, while my parents have gone off into Bristol. I'm enjoying my holiday so far when my father tells me that tomorrow, we are going to visit one of his work colleagues who lives to the north of Bristol. My mood immediately drops when I hear this news. However, it lifts again when he tells me that it's not far from the South Wales main line and that I will be able to go train spotting if I like, rather than sit in with the boring grown-ups!

So the next day we go to visit his work colleague who lives in a place called Winterbourne. When I look on a map I notice immediately that not only is it near the London Paddington to South Wales main line but it is also on a stretch of line where the Bristol to Birmingham Line runs along this stretch of track too. So not only will I see plenty of 'Westerns' and 'Hymeks', but also plenty of 'Peaks' on their way to and from the West Country. I end up sitting on an embankment with some of the local children having an exciting time seeing trains pass below me on a very busy stretch of line.

At the end of the day I was feeling very pleased with myself looking through all the numbers that I had 'copped'. The thought struck me though, 'Why don't they build a station along this stretch of line? It would be perfect for people living round here to get a train in all directions without having to go into Bristol?' Little did I know that someone somewhere had already thought of that and Bristol Parkway would be opened less than a year later, just a couple of miles further down the track. The rest, as they say, is history...

Almost 50 years later I still enjoy travelling by train, though the train spotting side of me departed in my mid-teens when girls and rock music took over. In the last ten years or so my interest in railways and travelling by train has reignited with retirement. As a result I have travelled all over the country from Penzance in Cornwall to Thurso in the far north of Scotland. This led me to starting the website Branch Line Britain, where I have catalogued all the railway branch lines plus many other minor lines. In fact I have grown to have a strong interest in the railway stations and routes side of things and Parkway stations is one of these interests.

I have tried to include as much detail as possible about each Parkway station including its history, services and destinations, and its *raison d'etre*. I also spent a year or so personally visiting each Parkway station, taking photographs, and noting the particular characteristics of each one.

The result is this book, which was originally delivered to the publishers in February 2020 with publication scheduled for summer 2020. However, the Coronavirus pandemic put paid to that and everything got delayed. It goes without saying that COVID-19 has had a devastating effect on Britain's railways and public transport system in general. With many people being urged by the government to work from home and not use public transport unless absolutely necessary, passenger numbers have plummeted to their lowest since the railways began.

Although there was a slight revival in numbers in August and September 2020 with lockdown restrictions being lifted, mainly in leisure travellers as opposed to commuters, numbers have once again gone down. As I write this, the rollout of the vaccination has started, which has given hope of an end to the pandemic, but when things will get back to normal is anyone's guess. It will take a long time for passengers to regain their trust in travelling by public transport and by train in particular, and for passenger numbers to reach their pre-COVID levels. In the meantime, I have included in this book details of where there has been an impact made by COVID, especially in regard to Airport Parkway stations.

Mark Chatterton
Essex
December 2020

CHAPTER 1

The Origin of the Name 'Parkway'

The whole concept of Parkway railway stations is bound up in the word 'Parkway'. So where does the word 'Parkway' actually come from? Many would say the term originated in the United States as far back as the 1800s when the first Parkway roads were built there. The first one constructed was Eastern Parkway in Brooklyn, New York City, which opened in 1874. That and the others which followed it were roadways where there was a wide area for pedestrians to walk along in a park-like setting with trees and grass, separate from the horse drawn vehicles and later motor traffic that used the road itself.

The name also came to refer to a road that was joined to, or which went through, a municipal park in some parts of the USA. As time went by, Parkway roads came to be more about a landscaped road with a strip of grass in the middle and tree-lined edges, where high speed traffic could travel along with the absence of pedestrians, who were now excluded from these types of roads. Indeed, there are several examples of this type of 'Parkway' road in UK cities such as London, Manchester, Peterborough, and Plymouth.

However, in the UK there is actually a place called 'Parkway', a small hamlet in Herefordshire, just south of Ledbury on the A417. Apparently, the name comes from 'Parkway Corner', which came in turn from nearby Dingwood Park, a late 17th century Grade II listed building, originally occupied by the Wall family. So, we can find the term 'Parkway', a whole 200 years before the Americans coined the term.

Just what has this got to do with Parkway railway stations though? Well, some believe that the first Parkway railway station, Bristol Parkway, comes from an area of parkland near to the station, with a walkway that you could walk through; hence the name 'Parkway' was chosen. So, it wasn't actually anything to do with parking your car and going away on a train somewhere—as many people thought and still do.

A first day cover celebrating the opening of Bristol Parkway, calling it the 'First Inter-City Motorway Railway Station'.

In fact the truth lies nearer the American meaning of the word. Bristol Parkway was originally going to be called 'Bristol North', but as it wasn't quite in Bristol in those days, it was felt that a more appropriate name was needed. The station in waiting was actually in the village of Stoke Gifford, which is the name of the goods yard next to it, but that wouldn't do either. So in the days of British Rail, someone from the Western Region organised a competition to find a suitable name. As it was near the northern end of the M32 motorway—which leads into central Bristol—and that motorway was known locally as 'The Parkway', someone thought 'Bristol Parkway' would be a suitable name. And so that is the name which was chosen above all the other entries. In fact some publicity for the new station called it a 'Motorway Railway Station' as it was so close to the three motorways!

Still, the name 'Parkway' stuck in the consciousness of the British public and came in time to be associated with an out of town Park and Ride type railway station that you could drive to, PARK your car (for free back then) and then catch a train to go aWAY somewhere, usually to work or to the shops; hence 'Parkway'.

CHAPTER 2

What is a Parkway railway station?

A Parkway railway station could be said to be a railway station that has been built specifically as a Park and Ride interchange for a wide area rather than to serve a particular town or village. The idea being that you drive your car to the station and park it there before taking a train to your destination. Previously, most people would arrive at their local station by foot, by bus or by taxi, or perhaps would be given a lift there by car.

Of course it could be argued that many of today's suburban railway stations, with their large car parks, cater for commuters in a similar way to Parkway railway stations, just without the 'Parkway' suffix. The reason there are so many of these stations catering mainly for commuters is this: up until the 1960s and even into the 1970s many railway stations still had a goods shed and sidings which were in use. Gradually with road transport taking over from railways in the delivery of small goods at least, these sheds and sidings became redundant and a car park was inevitably built on their site.

A Parkway station differs from this model in that it is usually built on a green field site, away from a town, sometimes 'in the middle of nowhere'. Proximity to a major road is also a factor. Most importantly of all, it is built as a railhead for the many villages and small towns that surround it, where walking or getting a bus to the station is not always an option and so the best way of accessing that Parkway station is by car. In order to cater for this type of customer, the station should have a largish car park (or two in some cases) which ideally is free to use – at least in the early days of Parkway stations it was! Of course there are exceptions to this rule where an existing railway station has become a Parkway railway station instead, such as at Didcot.

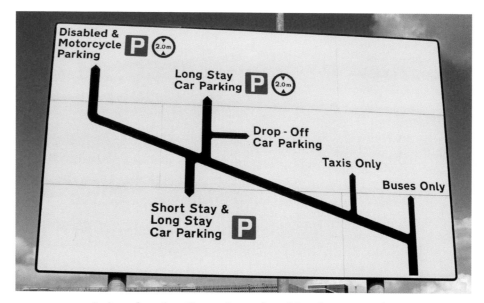

**A sign showing the variety of parking functions for
road vehicles at Bristol Parkway station.**

Where exactly in Great Britain are these Parkway stations situated? Well for a start they could all be said to be situated virtually to the west of London, many in the Home Counties. In fact almost half of them can be found in what might be called 'The Parkway Triangle', the points of which are Birmingham to the north, Bristol to the west and London to the east. The vast majority of Parkway stations are in England, with just two in Wales and none at all in Scotland. Within England there are only three in the North West and just two in the East Midlands, with the rest being at various points in a line roughly south of Birmingham. There are also two to be found in the Irish Republic.

PARKWAY STATION INGREDIENTS

What are the various factors or 'ingredients' needed for a parkway railway station? Firstly, it needs to be built on a railway line with good connections to a major town offering work, shopping or tourism destinations. In fact, it is possible to catch a direct train to London from 17 of the 22 existing Parkway stations. The rest are connected to other large cities such as Birmingham, Nottingham and Manchester.

This sign at East Midlands Parkway shows what a Parkway railway station is all about in a nutshell.

Secondly, it should have a large catchment area within easy driving distance. Many people who use Parkway stations to get to and from work, live in villages or small towns where car ownership is the norm and have sufficient income to pay for both the railway fare and the car parking charge. In addition, a Parkway station on the edge of a city, such as Oxford or Bristol, is a far more attractive proposition than using the city centre station.

Thirdly, a large car park with reasonable car parking charges is a must. Although Parkway station car parking was free in the early days, there are now just a handful of examples where this remains the case. Some of the newer Parkway stations have been built next to existing Park and Ride facilities, including those at Oxford and Stratford-upon-Avon, making them integrated transport interchanges.

Fourthly, it should have a regular and fairly frequent train service, such as every 20 minutes or every half hour. An hourly service is unlikely to be acceptable to most Parkway patrons.

Fifthly, it should have all the basic facilities expected of a train station, including a ticket office, toilets and café. It should also be compliant with the 2005 Disability Discrimination Act with either lifts or ramps in place.

Finally, there should be good local transport alternatives for non-car users including buses or taxis, as well as secure parking for bicycles or motorbikes.

HOW TO CREATE A PARKWAY STATION

Firstly, there must be an economic case for it - usually put forward by a local council or a county council or perhaps Network Rail. For example, new housing estates under construction near a railway line might result in enough demand to warrant a station.

Secondly, there must be plenty of space available, not only for the station platforms, but also for a station building and a large car park. There must also be enough room around the line for additional infrastructure, potentially including new signalling, a revised track layout and electrics.

Thirdly, the possibility of fitting stops at this new Parkway station into already busy route schedules must be assessed. For example, when Liverpool South Parkway was first opened not all the trains passing through stopped there. Eventually this changed when the train operating companies saw the demand for having a stop there.

Finally, and perhaps most crucially of all, there must be sufficient finance available to cover all the costs involved.

If all these hurdles can be overcome, then the ball can start to roll. The initial step might be a feasibility study for the project. Or there might be a council motion to support the station's construction. Detailed funding plans would need to be drawn up showing what would be required from each partner organisation involved in the project - no doubt including both the government and local councils. Furthermore, the public would need to be won over. There could conceivably be objections based on an increase in traffic in the area around the station, noise nuisance or even light pollution at night.

Once all these points have been addressed and resolved, work can begin on the site—surveying, clearing and finally laying the foundations of where the station building will be. The building of platforms might mean work taking place at night when there are no trains passing. Alternatively, the whole track in the area might have to be closed while this happens.

Even when everything has been built, rigorous safety checks and practice runs have to be made before train services can commence at the station. Then at last the station can open and the public can be notified through various media. If every step has been followed correctly, the station will most likely be a success!

CHAPTER 3

A History of Parkway Stations

Although Parkway stations did not come into existence until the 1970s, their roots can be found in the 1960s.

The decade was one of great change, with Britain gradually rebuilding itself after the ravages of the Second World War. Many towns were being rebuilt and redeveloped after bomb damage with large, covered shopping centres becoming the norm in city centres. The country's road network was extended far and wide — with dual carriageways and motorways forming the backbone of a co-ordinated road system. This slowly started taking more freight away from the railways. Car ownership increased as people found they had more disposable income. This meant fewer people travelling on the railways, which had been greatly reduced after the Beeching Report of 1963.

More cars meant more traffic jams, especially in town centres, and one way of reducing these was the concept of 'Park and Ride'. This was where you drove to a car park on the edge of a town then caught a bus into the town centre, avoiding the stress of finding a parking space and reducing traffic congestion. Oxford was the first place in the UK to operate such a system, though it was quite primitive in the early days — operating from a hotel car park in the 1960s. It only lasted a year and it wasn't until 1973 that a permanent Park and Ride facility was opened at Redbridge to the south of the city.

New Pudsey station looking east with a train to Hull on February 18, 2020.

Someone in the Eastern Region of British Railways may well have been paying close attention to this development because Britain's first purpose-built Park and Ride railway station was opened as 'New Pudsey' in West Yorkshire on March 6, 1967. Many see this as the 'first Parkway station ever built', even though it has never had the name 'Parkway' added to it.

This was a whole five years before Bristol Parkway opened and it certainly had a lot of the 'Parkway' idea about it. Situated between Bradford and Leeds, it was built on a large site which included a 200-plus capacity car park. It was near to the A6110, the Leeds Outer Ring Road, so accessibility for motorists was easy. When it first opened there was a direct service to London, which meant it was more convenient to drive to New Pudsey than the town centre stations of Bradford Exchange or Leeds City.

However, when the London service ended in 1988 the station lost its appeal for many and it became just another commuter station with a large car park. Incidentally, 'New Pudsey' does not exist. The station was not even in Pudsey, but rather in Farsley. As a concept, it was planned as a 'new station' for Pudsey.

Another business model taking off at this time, where car and train came together, was 'Motorail'. Here passengers could take their car with them on the train, usually going to some far-flung destination such as Scotland or the West Country. On arrival, they unloaded their car from the back of the train and off they went on their holiday. Motorail was a clever idea intended to take cars away from the motorway network and bring passengers back onto trains, but it peaked in the 1970s. If only you could get the motorist to leave their car at the railway station...

Five years after the opening of New Pudsey, the first 'named' Parkway station, 'Bristol Parkway', opened on May 1, 1972, at Stoke Gifford, to the north of Bristol. This was where the South Wales mainline from London to Cardiff converged with the Cross-Country route from the West of England to the North of England and Scotland.

It was a perfect choice of location because passengers could change trains onto routes that would not otherwise be possible. Plus, being situated near to where the M4 and M5 meet, and where the M32 coming out of Bristol meets up with the M4, it was sure to attract motorists using those motorways.

Finally, it was just to the north of Bristol—providing a huge potential customer base who might prefer to avoid going all the way into Bristol to catch a train at Temple Meads. Its success was guaranteed. The original two platforms have now been doubled to four and it has continued to be one of the busiest railway stations in the west of England.

Hot on its heels, another Parkway station was opened just a year later on May 7, 1973 at Alfreton, about 18 miles north of Nottingham. The 'Parkway' name must have struck a chord as it was called 'Alfreton and Mansfield Parkway'. The station was intended to attract passengers from the town of Mansfield nine miles away, which back then was the largest

A west bound train calls in at Bristol Parkway
shortly after opening in 1972. NEIL AVENTI

town in Britain without a railway station. However, the station became plain 'Alfreton' when Mansfield regained its own station in 1995 with the opening of the *Robin Hood Line* between Nottingham and Worksop. It has gradually increased its passenger numbers over the years and was used by more than 300,000 people in 2019/20.

Another Parkway type station, but without the suffix, opened in January 1976 as 'Birmingham International' at a site next to Birmingham Airport, which back then was known as 'Birmingham International Airport'. The following month the National Exhibition Centre opened

**Bodmin Parkway showing the station building on the right
and the former signal box, now a café, on the left.**

nearby, adding to its potential for attracting passengers. With direct
trains to London, Birmingham, Manchester, Glasgow, and Wales, it is
now one of the busiest railway stations in the West Midlands with just
over six and a half million passengers using it in 2019/20.

It could easily have been called 'Birmingham Parkway', being sited
next to the M42 and the A45 trunk road from Birmingham to Coventry,
though perhaps the suffix 'International' sounded better! Also in the
West Midlands, after a gap of seven years, a new Parkway station was
opened at Sandwell and Dudley in May 1983, although it didn't keep the
parkway suffix for long.

So far, all the Parkway stations to be opened had been built from
scratch, but in 1983 another Parkway station came into being, this time
at a railway station which had first opened in 1859. This was Bodmin
Parkway on the Cornish mainline between Plymouth and Penzance. It
had been known as Bodmin Road for over a hundred years, as it was
situated over three miles east of the town of Bodmin, which didn't get

A view along platform 2 to the west at Didcot Parkway station.

its own railway station, Bodmin General, until 1887. This had shut in 1967 and so Bodmin Road was its nearest railhead.

The name was changed to Bodmin Parkway in October 1987 to attract more users to the station—which had a car park to cater for motorists. It also had the advantage of local stopping trains to both Penzance and Plymouth as well as long distance express services to the likes of London, Birmingham, Manchester and Glasgow. Bodmin Parkway was the first of just a handful of existing railway stations to be redesignated as a Parkway station, though perhaps its location away from a large population has deterred other existing railway stations from following suit.

The first Parkway station in Wales was opened in December 1984. This time it was not situated away from a town but was actually in a town—namely Port Talbot. Following on from the success of the other Parkway stations it was named 'Port Talbot Parkway' in the hope of attracting customers from further down the M4, which ran along the north side of the town. Like Bodmin Parkway before it, the name was

**An East Midlands Trains service for London St Pancras
International at Luton Airport Parkway on March 23, 2019.**

applied to an old station which had been in existence since 1850. Port
Talbot Parkway still retains the name today and attracts over half a
million passengers a year.

Seven months later, in July 1985, yet another 'old station' and another
from the Western Region of British Railways changed its name to become
the sixth Parkway station, namely Didcot. Like Port Talbot, its name
came from the town next door, though there was a large catchment
area of smaller towns and villages quite close by. It offered passengers
a large selection of destinations, being at the junction of where the line
from Oxford and Birmingham joins up with the Great Western mainline to Bristol as well as Cardiff. It is now the second busiest Parkway
station in Britain.

Another Western Region Parkway station opened the following year, in May 1986, as Tiverton Parkway. This time it was a new build and replaced the nearby Tiverton Junction station. Like Bodmin Parkway, it was not only on the line from London Paddington to Penzance, but also on the Cross Country route to Birmingham and beyond. It had the advantage of being right next to junction 27 of the M5 where traffic coming from North Devon on the A361 joined the motorway.

A few months later the first Southern Region Parkway station opened north of Southampton, right next to Southampton Airport. It was initially called 'Southampton Parkway' as it was quite close to the M27 and M3 motorways, but in 1994 it became 'Southampton Airport Parkway' to emphasise its closeness to the airport. It became another Parkway station success, with getting on for two million passengers a year until the pandemic struck.

The first of several Parkway stations in the Chilterns area opened on the Chiltern mainline between London Marylebone and Birmingham Moor Street in October 1987. This was Haddenham & Thame Parkway and it provided a railway connection for the nearby town of Thame, which had lost its railway station in 1963. Opening it was a big risk as this line had been run down considerably by British Railways—and it was single track, with trains only going as far north as Banbury. Yet, on its opening day, hundreds of well wishers turned out to greet the first train. The station has benefited from privatisation with station buildings being added, the track redoubled and express trains now running once again between Marylebone and Birmingham. Almost a million passengers a year were using this Parkway station before the pandemic.

The second Parkway station in the West Midlands area was opened in June 1990 at Tame Bridge Parkway to the north of Birmingham in the West Bromwich area, almost next to the M5 and M6. Despite a lack of motorway access, and a reliance on local commuter traffic, it is still going strong 30 years later with over half a million passengers using it.

There were no further Parkway station openings during the early 1990s but November 1995 saw the East Midlands get its first Parkway railway

Liverpool South Parkway station sign emphasising the connection for Liverpool John Lennon Airport.

station, Sutton Parkway on the newly opened *Robin Hood Line* between Nottingham and Worksop. Built to serve the nearby town of Sutton-in-Ashfield, it is quite a small Parkway station compared to its predecessors, though passenger numbers are expected to eventually overtake the 200,000 a year mark.

Nearly four years passed before two more Parkway stations were opened in 1999. Perhaps this gap was due to the privatisation of Britain's railways taking place; most of the newly formed Train Operating Companies were still finding their feet. These next two were Horwich Parkway, near Bolton, and Luton Airport Parkway, to the north of London. The latter has been the busiest of all the Parkway stations with well over four million passengers using it in 2019/20, reflecting a growth in both airline passengers and rail passengers. Since COVID-19 happened this Parkway station, like several others, has seen a sharp decrease in passenger numbers. Whether it ever reaches the high figures it had pre-pandemic remains to be seen.

In October 2000, another Parkway station was opened on the Cotswold mainline at Warwick Parkway, near to the M40. This has been another successful Parkway station, partly due to its fast connections to both

Birmingham and London. Over half a million passengers were using it annually until COVID happened.

Liverpool South Parkway opened next, in June 2006. This was an amalgamation of two stations–Allerton and Garston on two different lines which cross over each other at this station. Although it is not near any motorway, it is the nearest railway station for Liverpool John Lennon Airport and so caters for those passengers. Since it has opened passenger numbers have grown steadily to almost 300,000 a year.

The following year, in May 2007, another 'old station' changed its name to become a Parkway station. This was Whittlesford, situated to the south of Cambridge near to the M11 motorway. It was the first Parkway station in East Anglia, and to date the only one. A month later came Coleshill Parkway to the east of Birmingham, followed by Ebbw Vale Parkway in February 2008, East Midlands Parkway in January 2009 and Aylesbury Vale Parkway in December 2009 — showing that the trend for opening Parkway stations was growing. All of them were 'new build' and both Ebbw Vale and Aylesbury were terminus stations which was a first, with both having just a single platform.

There was a gap of almost two years before Buckshaw Parkway to the south of Preston was opened in October 2011, followed by Stratford-up-on-Avon Parkway 18 months later in May 2013.

Then in October 2015 Oxford Parkway station was opened to the north of Oxford on a completely rebuilt stretch of line between Oxford and Bicester, which also connects with the Chiltern mainline. This allowed trains to go to Oxford from London Marylebone and when the line eventually reopens between Bicester and Bletchley they may well be able to go to Milton Keynes and Bedford.

Finally, in February 2020 the latest Parkway railway station to open was Worcestershire Parkway — where the Cotswold line goes over the Birmingham to Bristol mainline. With more Parkway stations being constructed or planned at places such as Portway Parkway, Cardiff Parkway and Rugby Parkway, it seems that the phenomena of Parkway stations will be with us for years to come.

CHAPTER 4

The Current Parkway Stations

For each Parkway station the following information has been included: After the name of the station, its three letter station code is given. The full postal address of the station and the date it opened to the public are also included.

The Train Operating Company that manages the station is given, alongside which company's trains use the station, as of December 2020.

All possible destinations that can be reached by train from the station have been stated, as of January 2021, as well as the number of platforms.

The frequency of off-peak trains is shown, based on pre-COVID levels.

The Department for Transport (DfT) category, where known, is shown. This is a letter ranging from A to F denoting how busy/important a particular railway station is. A is the busiest and F is the least busy. This was last reviewed in 2009.

The nearest town or towns and nearby roads are also cited.

Bus links show the numbers of the buses which call at or near to the station.

Finally, there is a trivia section where interesting or unusual facts about each Parkway station are presented.

Please note that the information given is deemed to be correct at the time of publication, though buses serving a particular station can change, as can the destination a train may go to.

Aylesbury Vale Parkway (AVP)

Address: Bicester Road, Aylesbury
HP18 0PS
Opened: December 14, 2009
Station building opened: June 1, 2010
Managed by: Chiltern Railways
**Train Operating Company using the
station:** Chiltern Railways
Destinations: Aylesbury, London
Marylebone

Frequency of off-peak trains: Hourly
Number of platforms: 1
DfT category: E
Nearest town: Aylesbury
Nearby roads: A41, A413, A418
Bus links: 4/4A Green Route, 16
Trivia: Aylesbury Vale Parkway is
the only Parkway station that is a
terminus station.

A view looking down the single platform at Aylesbury Vale Parkway
station on January 28, 2020. The former Great Central line is to the right.

HISTORY

The railway line that runs alongside Aylesbury Vale Parkway station was once part of the Great Central Railway that ran from London Marylebone to Manchester Piccadilly. It also had the trains of the Metropolitan Line using the same track as far as Quainton Road and then onto Verney Junction. Passenger services north of Aylesbury station ceased in September 1966 though the line was left open for freight workings and the occasional special train.

It wasn't until the start of the 21st century that things changed. Firstly, Aylesbury as a regional town for this part of Buckinghamshire was growing rapidly with several new housing estates being built to the north and east of the town. Secondly, with no bypass, traffic moving through the town was often delayed due to congestion and the idea of a Park and Ride station on the outskirts of the town seemed like a good idea.

Plans for a new station to the north of Aylesbury to serve the communities of Berryfields and Haydon Hill was approved by the government in 2006. £8.17 million in funding came from the office of the Deputy Prime Minister which was to improve track and signalling on the line north of Aylesbury station. This would allow Chiltern Railways to build a new Parkway station on a site just off the A41, about three miles north west of Aylesbury town centre. Chiltern Railways would contribute £2.8 million, and Buckinghamshire County Council another £1 million. With work due to start in 2007, the station was expected to open in 2010. In fact Chiltern started operating a service in December 2009, with the station building and surrounding infrastructure being opened in June 2010.

OVERVIEW

Aylesbury Parkway railway station is situated by the A41 Aylesbury to Bicester Trunk Road. It is surrounded by new housing developments with more planned at the time of writing. It has direct trains to London Marylebone via Amersham and is about three miles north of Aylesbury train station.

The station building at Aylesbury Vale Parkway station.

There is a railway line that passes the station at the moment which is used by 'Bin Liner' waste disposal trains. These carry on to Calvert, a landfill waste area, a further eight miles up the line. However this line does go on to join the old 'Varsity Line' running between Oxford and Bedford at Claydon Junction, approximately seven miles east of Bicester Village station. Trains to London Marylebone take around one hour 10 minutes to complete the journey, though the fastest is timed at one hour three minutes. In the opposite direction, trains usually take one hour six minutes, with the fastest being one hour one minute, so it is an ideal commuter station.

Although the station has a ticket office, toilets and waiting area, at present this shuts just before midday and doesn't open until early the next morning. There are plenty of parking spaces and bicycle storage spaces as well as a taxi rank. There is a bus service running roughly every 15 minutes into the Berryfields Estate and back into Aylesbury. Perhaps if the extra platforms are ever built (see below) the station may be busier during the day and not just at peak times.

FUTURE PLANS

In February 2020 it was announced that the go ahead had been given by for the line between Aylesbury Parkway and Claydon Junction to be upgraded. This could eventually result in an hourly train service between Aylesbury and Milton Keynes and Oxford. If this happens, two more platforms would be added to the station on the side where the through track is.

Bodmin Parkway (BOD)

(CORNISH — FORDH BOSVENA)

Address: Station Approach, off Liskeard Road, near Bodmin, Cornwall PL30 4BB

Opened: June 27, 1859 as Bodmin Road. Changed name to Bodmin Parkway on November 4, 1983

Managed by: Great Western Railway

Train Operating Companies using the station: Bodmin & Wenford Railway, Cross Country, Great Western Railway

Destinations: Bodmin General, Boscarne Junction, Cardiff Central, Exeter St Davids, London Paddington, Newcastle, Penzance, Plymouth

Frequency of off-peak trains: one train every two hours to London Paddington, two trains per hour to Penzance and Plymouth

Number of platforms: 3

DfT category: D

Nearest town: Bodmin

Nearby road: A38

Bus links: 11, 11A, 176

Trivia: Bodmin Parkway is the only Parkway station to have a connecting platform for a preserved railway line, namely the Bodmin & Wenford Railway.

The picturesque footbridge dominates this scene of Bodmin Parkway station looking west in April 2019.

HISTORY

The Cornish mainline from Plymouth to Penzance was opened in May 1859, followed by the station called 'Bodmin Road' a month later. As the mainline bypassed Bodmin this was the nearest place where a station could be built. This line and much of the Great Western Railway at the time was built with broad gauge track, which was in use until 1892 when standard gauge replaced it.

It wasn't until May 1887 that Bodmin town was linked to Bodmin Road. This was built with standard gauge, so until the broad gauge on the mainline was replaced by standard gauge, goods and passengers had to change trains at Bodmin Road until through trains were able to proceed.

The station remained as Bodmin Road until November 4, 1983, when it became 'Bodmin Parkway', the fourth station be given the Parkway title.

OVERVIEW

Bodmin Parkway is a pleasant parkway station on the Cornish main-line between Plymouth and Penzance. The most noticeable aspect of this

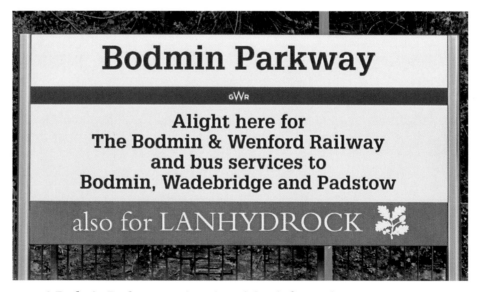

A Bodmin Parkway station sign giving information to passengers of local bus services and nearby tourist attractions.

station is the black and white painted footbridge which is the oldest part of the station along with the original Victorian-built signal box on the down platform. This has been preserved on site as a cafe. The original Victorian station buildings were demolished in 1989, six years after the station had been renamed. They were replaced with the present waiting room and ticket office building on the same platform.

On the other platform, an island platform, passengers can catch a steam train into Bodmin itself, courtesy of the Bodmin and Wenford Railway which operates trains out of this Parkway station. It is also close to Lanhydrock House, a 17th century stately home and this is shown on the station signs. There is a waiting room on this platform for westbound passengers. The station is near to the A38 but is accessed via a narrow lane. There is a car park with 70 spaces next to the station.

FUTURE PLANS

In 2019 the 'Barrow Crossing' right of less able passengers to cross over the line at the western end of the station to reach the island platform was withdrawn. Being such an old station, with no lifts or ramps, this has caused problems for those in wheelchairs, etc. — the only option being to use the stairs. Perhaps the introduction of lifts here might be the solution?

The car park is also limited to 70 spaces, which in summer soon fills up. Plus there is no room to park on the narrow approach road from the A38. A possible solution might be to add another level to the car park as has been done at Haddenham and Thame Parkway, and many other railway stations. This would double the number of spaces available and lead to more people using the station.

Bristol Parkway (BPW)

Address: Station Approach Road, off Hatchet Road, Stoke Gifford, City of Bristol BS34 8PU

Opened: May 1, 1972

Managed by: Great Western Railway

Train Operating Companies using the station: Cross Country, Great Western Railway

Destinations: Birmingham New Street, Brighton, Bristol Temple Meads, Carmarthen, Dundee, Frome, Gloucester, Great Malvern, Leeds, London Paddington, Penzance, Plymouth, Portsmouth & Southsea, Swansea, Warminster, Westbury, Weston-Super-Mare, Weymouth, Worcester Foregare Street, Worcester Shrub Hill

Frequency of off peak trains: two trains per hour to Cardiff and London, two trains per hour to Birmingham New Street, one of which goes to Manchester Piccadilly and one goes to Edinburgh, four trains per hour to Bristol Temple Meads

Number of platforms: 4

DfT category: B

Nearest towns: Bristol, Yate

Nearby roads: A38, A4174, M4, M5, M32

Bus links: 10, 11, 12, 19, 73, Y6

Trivia: The actual name for the station 'Bristol Parkway' was chosen by a member of the public in a competition organised by British Rail Western Region.

A view of Bristol Parkway station building and car park shortly after opening in 1972. NEIL AVENTI

HISTORY

The line on which Bristol Parkway station is situated opened as late as 1903 when the Great Western Railway opened the 'Badminton Line', running from the west of Swindon to Patchway to the west of Bristol Parkway. It was designed as a short cut from the original Great Western mainline from London to Cardiff which ran through Bristol Temple Meads.

The line between Bristol and Gloucester began life in July 1844 as part of the Bristol and Gloucester Railway, which eventually became part of the Midland Railway through to Birmingham. This line went to the north east of Bristol via Fishponds and trains used this route well into British Railways days until 1970. After that date, Birmingham to Bristol trains were diverted to use the Badminton Line and the line from Westerleigh Junction was closed.

The idea of having a station on this section of the line was seen as an alternative Bristol station for the residents of north Bristol. Plus, it was near to the M4, M5 and M32 motorways, which could also attract patrons.

Bristol Parkway was opened on May 1, 1972, on the site of the former Stoke Gifford marshalling yard which closed in October 1971 so the station could be built. It was seen as the first of a new generation of Park and Ride stations, though some would argue that New Pudsey near Bradford deserved that accolade. It was originally going to be called Bristol North or even Stoke Gifford in the planning stages before the British Railways Western Region competition which produced the name 'Bristol Parkway'.

The original station was built by Stone & Co of Bristol with a single storey building housing the ticket office and a waiting room. This first incarnation of Bristol Parkway station was very basic with open platforms each having a single bus style shelter. The platforms were connected by an open footbridge.

On either side of the platform were through tracks. Canopies were added to both platforms in 1973, as well as the footbridge being covered over. The associated car park was big enough to hold up to 600 cars and was free for several years to attract passengers to the station. The first trains could reach London Paddington in 95 minutes, but with the introduction of the High Speed Trains in 1976 the journey time was reduced to 75 minutes.

Over the years the station has been improved and redeveloped. In 2000 the Royal Mail opened a mail terminal on the east side of the station, which meant that some of the car park was lost. However it closed only four years later when the Royal Mail stopped using it and it was demolished in 2007. In its place was built a Network Rail maintenance training centre.

The station was redeveloped in 2000-2001, with a completely new station building fit for the 21st century including lifts, a café, waiting area and toilets. A third platform was opened in 2007, followed by a fourth in 2018. Electrification through the station was completed at the end of 2018.

This sign gives information to passengers on all the different facilities available at Bristol Parkway station.

OVERVIEW

Bristol Parkway station is in the north of Bristol where the South Wales mainline from London Paddington to Swansea and the Bristol to Birmingham line run together for about five miles before going their separate ways. It is also situated within a few miles of three motorways—the M4, the M5 and the M32, as well as the A38 and the A4174, providing easy access for motorists.

An overall view of the front entrance to Bristol Parkway with the multi-storey car park on the left and the station platforms on the right. The station building in the centre was opened in 2001.

The current station building dates from 2001 and like many modern station buildings features a lot of concrete and stainless steel. The station building is in fact on three levels with the platform level being high up and the waiting area/ticket office being on the ground floor. The buffet area and newsagents are also on the top floor. There is a large multi-storey car park to the north of the station and a large dropping off area/bus stop right in front of the station. There is another car park on the other side of the station building too and in all there are more than 1100 car parking spaces available—the greatest capacity of any parkway station. There is storage for around 150 bicycles as well. All four platforms have waiting rooms. To the south of the platforms there is a large yard where freight trains are stored.

FUTURE PLANS

Since the line through the station was electrified in 2018, train times have improved. As from December 2019 a fast direct train service to London Paddington started running nonstop to the capital. At just one hour 10 minutes there were several of these trains introduced throughout the day. No doubt this will lead to the demand for more parking spaces, so perhaps more room will have to be found at the station.

The Bristol Metro scheme planned for introduction over the next few years utilising the Henbury Loop Line may include trains from Bristol Parkway. If it does, extra platform capacity will have to be found. Some have suggested having a fifth platform by the former post office terminal on the north side of the station and this would certainly help.

Buckshaw Parkway (BSV)

Address: Station Approach, Buckshaw Village, Lancashire PR7 7EY

Opened: October 3, 2011

Managed by: Northern Trains

Train Operating Company using the station: Northern Trains

Destinations: Blackpool North, Hazel Grove, Manchester Airport, Manchester Victoria, Preston

Frequency of off peak trains: 3 trains per hour to Preston, 2 of which continue to Blackpool North, 1 train per hour to Manchester Victoria, 1 train per hour to Manchester Airport, 1 train per hour to Hazel Grove

Number of platforms: 2

Nearest towns: Chorley, Preston

Nearby roads: A49, A6, M6, M61

Bus links: 109, 415, 804, 810

Trivia: It took over ten years from planning permission being given to the station actually being opened, mainly due to lack of funds.

Buckshaw Parkway station building.

HISTORY

The line from Manchester to Preston originally opened in stages between 1838 and 1841. For many years there was a station near to the present Buckshaw Parkway station in the village of Euxton. This was the station for the Royal Ordnance Factory, which was situated on land either side of the railway just to the south of Buckshaw Parkway.

The factory at its peak employed more than 40,000 workers, making a nearby station a necessity. This was known as Chorley RDF Platform and was opened in 1938 with four platforms. It was later renamed as plain Chorley Halt in 1942 and lasted until 1963 when it was closed. The station site remained in situ for many years and was eventually cleared in the 2000s. Once the factory closed the site was redeveloped for housing and light industry, resulting in a considerable increase in Euxton's population to around 10,000.

With the building of the Buckshaw housing development, one of the largest urban developments in the North West, the need for a new station to cater for the expanding population grew. Planning permission for the station was originally given in 1999, but the building was delayed when it was found that there was a funding shortfall.

It was only in 2009 that work was able to proceed when £3.3 million from the Community Investment Fund was allocated to the scheme by Lancashire County Council. Construction should have started in early 2010, but another funding shortfall led to the design of the ticket office being changed. Work finally started in October 2010 and the station was opened a year later on October 3, 2011. This two-platform station cost almost £7 million on completion.

Further developments happened when it was announced that the line would be electrified in 2014. Work started to electrify the line in May 2015 but due to problems with subsidence caused by old mine workings on parts of the line, it wasn't completed until December 2018 when the first test trains ran. The first passenger services using scheduled electric Class 319 units started on February 11, 2019.

A Class 319 electric multiple unit at Buckshaw Parkway
on June 8, 2019 with a southbound service.

OVERVIEW

Buckshaw Parkway is one of the more modern parkway stations, being less than ten years old. It still has a new look about it with a neat one storey station building. Inside you will find a ticket office, waiting area, baby changing room and toilets. It is surrounded by the new houses of Buckshaw Village (pop. 4000) and a large supermarket. The car park has 200 free spaces with 10 spaces for bicycles. Outside there is a taxi rank and a community notice board, which is a nice touch.

The station lies on the recently electrified mainline from Manchester to Preston. From the station you can either go north to Preston and Blackpool, or south to central Manchester, Manchester Airport or Hazel Grove.

FUTURE PLANS

Apart form an increase in car parking spaces to cope with the increased use of the station, there are not really any future developments for the station. As it is predominantly a commuter type station catering for people working mainly in Manchester, but also Bolton and Preston, passengers wishing to go further afield can easily change trains at either Manchester or Preston.

Coleshill Parkway (CEH)

Address: Station Road, Coleshill, Warwickshire B46 1JZ

Opened: February 10, 1842, as Forge Mill. Renamed Coleshill in 1923. Closed July 4, 1968. Reopened as Coleshill Parkway June 19, 2007

Managed by: West Midlands Trains

Train Operating Company using the station: Cross Country

Number of platforms: 2

Destinations: Birmingham New Street, Cambridge, Leicester, Stansted Airport

Frequency of off peak trains: half hourly to Birmingham and Leicester, with hourly trains going on to Stansted Airport

DfT category: E

Nearest town: Coleshill

Nearby roads: A446, M42, M6, M6 Toll

Bus links: 75, 75A, X70 Platinum

Trivia: Coleshill Parkway won the local council award for 'Contribution to the Local Economy' in 2008.

Coleshill Parkway station building with its distinctive square lift tower roof coverings.

HISTORY

The station that was originally on the site now occupied by Coleshill Parkway station was opened in February 1842 as Forge Mills station by the Birmingham and Derby Junction Railway. It was on the line between Birmingham Lawley Street and Whitacre Junction, which went onto Tamworth and ultimately Derby. The station was renamed 'Forge Mills and Coleshill' on November 1, 1849. Then on April 1, 1904, it went back to plain, 'Forge Mills'. It stayed this way for almost 20 years until July 9, 1923, when the London, Midland and Scottish Railway took over the route and it became 'Coleshill'.

Coleshill station functioned here for over 40 years until it was closed down on March 4, 1968. Although Coleshill was a typical country station serving the nearby village of Coleshill, it did have a small goods yard, which closed down in 1964. Near to the station was a gasification plant which was built in the 1960s and had its own sidings. This has now been demolished.

Also near to the station site are the Hams Hall Distribution Park and Rail Freight Terminal, the latter being accessed just east of the station.

Coleshill Parkway station was opened on September 18, 2007, by the then Transport Secretary, Rosie Winterton. It was built in response to the need for a Park and Ride station facility on the eastern edge of Birmingham near to the M42 and M6 motorways, the Ham Hall Distribution Park and the Birmingham Airport and the NEC. It was funded jointly by the department for Transport, Warwickshire County Council, North Warwickshire Borough Council and Laing Rail at a cost of £9 million.

OVERVIEW

Although Coleshill Parkway station has been in existence for well over ten years, it still looks quite new, featuring distinctive red brick lift shafts with large flat roofs. It is situated about nine miles east of Birmingham on the Birmingham to Leicester line, with the Hams Hall ABP Rail Freight Terminal to the north of the station. There are two car

**A view looking east at Coleshill Parkway station. Hams Hill
Distribution Park is to the left of the photograph.**

parks on the north side of the station with spaces for more than 200
cars, plus spaces for 20 bicycles. The car park was free until 2019, when
a charge was introduced.

The station is surrounded by factories on both sides, but if you go
further south beyond the factories there are some new housing estates
within walking distance of the railway station. There are two platforms
which each have a bus stop type shelter. The main building, which houses
the ticket office and a small waiting area, is on south side of the station.

It is quite a functional Parkway station, mainly catering for commuters
who go to work in Birmingham. There are just four trains per hour using
the station for most of the day, with two in each direction. Destinations

available are limited by the fact that the main Cross Country route between the West of England and the East Midlands bypasses the station on a nearby line to the west and north of the station.

FUTURE PLANS

There is not much to say about future plans for the station. It is served by a wide variety of buses to places such as Birmingham City Centre and the airport. It might benefit from some Cross Country trains between Birmingham and Derby being re-routed via the station to give a wider choice of through destinations from Coleshill Parkway.

Didcot Parkway (DID)

Address: Station Road, Didcot, Oxfordshire OX11 7NR

Opened: June 12, 1844, as Didcot. Changed name to Didcot Parkway on July 29, 1985

Managed by: Great Western Railway

Train Operating Company using the station: Great Western Railway

Destinations: Banbury, Bristol Temple Meads, Cheltenham Spa, London Paddington, Moreton In Marsh, Oxford, Reading, Swansea, Taunton, Weston-super-Mare

Frequency of off peak trains: five trains per hour to London Paddington, two trains per hour to Bristol Temple Meads and to Oxford, one train per hour to Cheltenham Spa

Number of platforms: 5

DfT category: B

Nearest towns: Didcot, Oxford, Wantage

Nearby roads: A4130, A34

Bus links: 33 Connector, 91, 94, 94S, 96, 98 Connector, 98A Connector, D1, D2, X2 Connector, X32 Connector, X33 Connector

Trivia: Didcot Parkway is the oldest Parkway railway station on the railway network in terms of having a station continuously on the same site since 1844.

Didcot Parkway station looking east with a Cross Country train in the platform. This was taken in February 2014 when floods had blocked the line between Didcot Parkway and Oxford so Cross Country trains from the south had to terminate at Didcot.

HISTORY

Didcot station, as it was originally called, opened on June 12, 1844, when a line to Oxford was built from the junction on the mainline. This route from London Paddington had been opened as far west as Steventon, about three miles beyond Didcot in June 1840 by the Great Western Railway. The original intention was to continue the line to Oxford from Steventon via the town of Abingdon. However there were objections to this route from the people of Abingdon so a route north from Didcot was chosen instead.

Another line was opened from Didcot in the 1880s by the Didcot, Newbury and Southampton Railway which went south to Newbury and Winchester, providing an important freight route from the Midlands to the port of Southampton, which added to the town's continued growth. It never quite achieved its potential though and was closed to passengers in 1962 and to freight in 1967.

However, with Didcot being on the Great Western mainline to Bristol and South Wales, as well as being the junction station for the route north to Oxford and Birmingham, it thrived throughout the 20th century. With the introduction of the High Speed Trains in the 1970s journey times to both London and Bristol were cut so more people in and around the town started using Didcot as a commuter station.

The original station building was replaced by a new building housing a ticket office, waiting area and a shop in 1985. A former provender store to the west of the station was demolished, releasing a large area of land where a car park was built. When the new station building and car park were opened by David Mitchell MP, the Parliamentary under Secretary of State for Transport, on July 29, the station was renamed 'Didcot Parkway'.

OVERVIEW

Didcot Parkway is the second busiest of all the Parkway stations with more than three million passengers using it in 2019/20. This is partly

A view of the front of Didcot Parkway station.

due to it being a busy interchange and partly due to the wide area it serves including the Culham Science Centre. The station front is quite impressive with a wide triangular frontage and there is plenty of room for buses to park in front of the station.

Didcot Parkway is the second biggest of the Parkway stations in terms of platform numbers, having five. On the far side of the station, looking north, you have a view of Didcot Railway Centre and indeed there is access from the station direct into the centre, avoiding a long walk around the station.

Over the years the number of car park spaces has increased and there are now more than 1100, with 226 cycle spaces. There is also a regular shuttle bus between the station and the Science Park.

FUTURE PLANS

The East West Rail project had included Didcot Parkway in its plans, where passengers using its trains could change trains here for Bristol Temple Meads and South Wales, but in 2020 planned services were changed to terminate at Oxford instead. At present Cross Country trains do not stop at the station, so passengers travelling from the Banbury and Oxford areas to these places have either to change trains at Oxford and then Didcot Parkway, or double back on themselves from Reading where they can change trains. This is something that needs to be addressed.

East Midlands Parkway (EMD)

Address: Station Approach Road off A453, Remembrance Way, near Ratcliffe-on-Soar, Nottinghamshire NG11 0EE

Opened: January 26, 2009

Managed by: East Midlands Railway

Train Operating Company using the station: East Midlands Railway

Destinations: Derby, Leeds, Leicester, London St Pancras International, Lincoln, Nottingham, Norwich, Sheffield

Frequency of off peak trains: 2 per hour to London, 1 per hour to Sheffield and 2 per hour to Nottingham, one of which goes on to Lincoln

Number of platforms: 4

DfT category: C1

Nearest towns: Derby, Loughborough, Nottingham

Nearby roads: A453, M1

Bus links: 865, MP3

Trivia: East Midlands Parkway is one of Britain's greenest railway stations having a geo-thermal heating system.

The vast cooling towers of Ratcliffe-on-Soar power station dominate the skyline at East Midlands Parkway station.

HISTORY

The Midland Main Line which runs between London St Pancras and Sheffield was opened in different stages, mainly during the years 1839 to 1868. The first section to be opened was between Derby and Nottingham in 1839, followed by the line south from Trent Junction to Leicester the following year. It wasn't until 1885 that the Midland Main Line as it is known today was finally completed. The Midland Main Line over the years has provided express trains between London and the East Midlands cities of Leicester, Derby and Nottingham, as well as to Sheffield in South Yorkshire. With the closure of the Great Central Main Line in 1966, the Midland Main Line became the only line from London to these cities.

Work started on a new railway station just south of Trent Junction in December 2007. The station would be called 'East Midlands Parkway' and was aimed at attracting passengers from the south side of Derby and Nottingham going south to London, as well as passengers using the East Midlands Airport, just four miles away. The project had been stuck in the planning stages for some years due to problems acquiring the land needed for the project. The station finally opened on January 26, 2009, after several delays.

In August 2019 the East Midlands Trains franchise was replaced by East Midlands Railway. One of the different services introduced was earlier trains between Sheffield/Nottingham to East Midlands Parkway.

OVERVIEW

East Midlands Parkway is in many ways the perfect parkway station — in theory at least. It is on an out-of-town site, with plenty of parking spaces and it is ideally placed just to the south of where the Midland Main Line splits in to four tracks. From west to east, tracks go off to Stoke-on-Trent, Derby, Sheffield via the Erewash Valley line and finally to Nottingham and Lincoln. To the south is Leicester and eventually London, which is only just over an hour and a half away. East Midlands Airport is four miles away, while the suburbs of Nottingham are just five miles away.

So on paper it should be a successful Parkway station with continuous growth in its ten years of existence. Yet in reality this hasn't happened. Although in its first year of operation more than 250,000 passengers used the station, beating predictions; East Midlands Trains then hoped to double that number within five years. Numbers did rise over the next few years, but not as high as expected.

Unlike most of the other parkway stations, where passenger numbers have grown steadily, usage of this station has been fairly level at around the 300,000 plus mark. In fact the number of passengers using the station has declined for two of the last three years.

Class 222 *Meridian* HST, No. 222012 takes the late running 12.45 service to London St Pancras, past Class 43 HST, No. 43049 on the 13.00 Nottingham service at East Midlands Parkway on March 23, 2019.

It would seem that the station's growth has been closely aligned to the growth of passenger numbers at East Midlands Airport. The number of passengers using the airport peaked in 2008 and since then has continued to decrease, perhaps linking to those using the station. Although there was a regular shuttle service between the airport and the station, this has now stopped. Also, the lack of any housing nearby may have been a factor in the lack of growth of passengers. Certainly East Midlands Parkway does not seem to have reached its potential yet.

Facilities seem to have been built with large numbers of passengers in mind. There is quite a large waiting room set out with rows of seats all looking at the information screen. The main hallway is quite big with a newsagents/coffee shop in one corner and a few tables and chairs next to it. There is a ticket office on the left as you go in which is open all through the day, and there are toilets on the right, plus there is a section in the middle with tables and chairs for customers of the café. The car park outside can cater for 850 vehicles.

The station is well served by trains though, with regular services to Leicester, London, Nottingham, Lincoln, Derby and Sheffield throughout the day. There is an early morning weekday through service to Norwich as well. Perhaps the fact that the two London trains each hour leave within ten minutes of each other and the fast trains to Nottingham and Sheffield also leave within seven minutes of each other does put potential passengers off.

Finally, the station has been built right next to Ratcliffe-on-Soar power station, with its cooling towers dominating the skyline. This is due to be decommissioned by 2025 and so these will have to be demolished eventually. Some people have speculated that the land may be used for housing which would benefit the station.

FUTURE PLANS

The main need for the station is to increase passenger numbers which should be a lot higher than they are. Perhaps if the departure pattern of some of the trains were changed, especially the two London trains which leave at 44 and 56 past the hour, then passenger numbers could increase.

Also, more could be made of its closeness to Donington Park Race Circuit which puts on not only racing events, but also music festivals. If there were shuttle buses/coaches operating from the station on event days then passenger numbers would surely increase.

Finally, if passenger air travel from the East Midlands airport recovers after COVID, increased numbers may affect passengers using the station, but only if better airport shuttle services are put into place.

Ebbw Vale Parkway (EBV)

(WELSH — GORSAF REILFFORDD PARCFFORDD GLYN EBWY)

Address: off Glen Ebbw Terrace, Waun-Lywd, Blaneau Gwent NP23 8AP

Opened: February 6, 2008

Managed by: Transport for Wales

Train Operating Company using the station: Transport for Wales

Destinations: Cardiff Central, Ebbw Vale Town, Milford Haven

Frequency of off peak trains: 1 train per hour to Cardiff and 1 train per hour to Ebbw Vale Town

Number of platforms: 1

Dft Category: F1

Nearest town: Ebbw Vale

Nearby road: A4046

Bus links: 98, E3

Trivia: Ebbw Vale Parkway is the smallest of all the Parkway stations on Britain's railway network with just one platform. It is also the least used parkway station with just 44,100 recorded entries and exits in the year 2019/20.

Ebbw Vale Parkway Station looking south on June 26, 2011, when the station was the terminus of the line. A Class 150 'Sprinter' two-car unit, No. 150255 waits to return to Cardiff Central.

HISTORY

Ebbw Vale Parkway lies on what was for many years a busy freight line. It was one of many to be found in the South Wales Valleys north of the ports of Cardiff and Newport, where the coal mined in the Valleys was shipped out around the world. The line between Newport and Ebbw Vale Town had first opened to passengers in 1850 and was eventually closed to passenger traffic in April 1962. The line was again reopened for passengers as far as Ebbw Vale Parkway in February 2008 after the line was doubled between Risca and Crosskeys. It was then extended to Ebbw Vale Town in May 2015.

OVERVIEW

Ebbw Vale Parkway station was the terminus of the newly opened passenger line along the Ebbw Valley before the May 2015 extension. Apart from Aylesbury Vale Parkway it is the only parkway station with a single platform. There is a shelter on the platform containing a ticket machine, plus there is an electronic information display board and help point on the platform. Beyond the station there is a 100 space free car park.

Passenger numbers have declined quite drastically at the station since the line was extended to Ebbw Vale Town. In 2014/15 there were 254,000 passengers using the station. Yet in 2018/19 the number was just 38,834, though the figure did rise again the following year to over 44,000. However, the effect of the pandemic has meant numbers will again be down.

At present there is just one train an hour to Ebbw Vale Town which terminates there and then returns down the valley to Cardiff and occasionally to Bridgend. So the current service is basic to say the least. If the line is doubled south of the station between Aberbeeg and Crosskeys and they start running trains to Newport, then things will no doubt pick up.

The villages of Victoria and Waun-Lwyd are to the south of the station, and these are now the station's main customers. Perhaps it would

**A bilingual commemorative plaque at Ebbw Vale Parkway
railway station showing the various stakeholders
involved in the project to open the station.**

probably be better calling the station 'Victoria' now that it no longer
serves the function of a Parkway railway station.

FUTURE PLANS

The line was meant to be doubled to the south in 2018 between Aberbeeg and Crosskeys to enable trains to run direct into Newport. This
has been put back to 2021, so until this happens it looks like Ebbw Vale
Parkway will continue to lose passengers. It does have a future, but only
as a local station for the communities nearby, rather than as a Parkway
station.

Haddenham & Thame Parkway (HDM)

Address: Thame Road, Haddenham, Buckinghamshire HP17 8EP

Opened: October 3, 1987

Managed by: Chiltern Railways

Train Operating Company using the station: Chiltern Railways

Destinations: Banbury, Birmingham Moor Street, Birmingham Snow Hill, High Wycombe, London Marylebone, Oxford, Stratford-upon-Avon

Frequency of off peak trains: 2 trains per hour to London Marylebone, 1 train per hour to Oxford, 1 train per hour to Banbury. Also to Birmingham, Stratford-upon-Avon and Kidderminster in peak hours

Number of platforms: 2

DfT category: E

Nearest towns: Aylesbury, Haddenham, Oxford, Thame

Nearby roads: A4129, A418, M40

Bus links: 111, 112, 120, 280, 280 Sapphire

Trivia: When the station building was rebuilt in 2014 at a cost of half a million pounds, it was opened by celebrity chef Raymond Blanc, who has a restaurant in the vicinity.

The station building at Haddenham & Thame Parkway railway station.

HISTORY

The line on which Haddenham & Thame Parkway stations is situated runs between London Marylebone and Birmingham Moor Street. It was opened in different stages primarily by the Great Western Railway, whose main route between London and Birmingham went via Oxford.

In the early 1900s a section of missing line between Princes Risborough and Banbury was constructed to bridge the gap and speed up train times. It came to be called the 'Bicester Cut-off' and meant a 20 minute saving of train times between Birmingham and London via this route. The line first opened to freight traffic on November 20, 1905, and then to passengers on April 2, 1906.

Haddenham station was the only station to be opened on this new

A Class 165 *Networker* unit No 165028 waits to depart from Haddenham & Thame Parkway station with a service for Banbury on a snowy February 1, 2019.

stretch of track, though Bicester North was eventually opened on July 1, 1910. The original Haddenham station was built about half a mile to the south east of the present Haddenham & Thame Parkway station and stayed open until January 7, 1963.

The line became single track in the late 1960s under British Rail when the West Coast mainline was electrified and traffic declined. However it was doubled again during the years 1998-2002 as part of 'Project Evergreen'. Haddenham & Thame Parkway station opened on October 3, 1987, and such was the interest in the new station that hundreds of people turned out for the opening. British Rail Network South East established it to provide a railhead for passengers from the town of Thame (pop. 11,000) four miles to the west, and for the residents of the village of Haddenham (pop. 4500).

With privatisation of Britain's railways in the 1990s the line was taken over by Chiltern Railways, which still manages the station and line today. In 1998, on the doubling of the track, the station was rebuilt in parts with a new southbound platform being added and new shelters installed, as well as a station building housing a ticket office and waiting room. This was extended further in 2014.

OVERVIEW

Haddenham & Thame Parkway station is a typical commuter Parkway station on the London Marylebone to Birmingham Snow Hill main line. A peak time train takes around 30 minutes nonstop to get you to the capital. Situated just four miles from the Oxfordshire town of Thame and right next to the village of Haddenham, it is a perfect station for commuters wishing to catch trains into the capital or to Oxford. Since the station was opened in 1987 the village of Haddenham has grown considerably, as has the number of passengers using the station. In 2018/19 almost a million passengers used the station, which reflects a year on year growth. The impact of COVID has led to a sharp drop in passenger numbers using the station, though it is thought that numbers will eventually rise again, but probably not to pre pandemic levels.

Although the station was opened over 30 years ago, it has all the facilities that you would expect from a modern station including ramps leading to the platforms, a large covered waiting shelter on the London bound platform and a large station building opposite. This contains a ticket office, waiting room and a café. The car park on the west side of the station now has over 700 spaces — originally it had 130 — with 100 bicycle spaces nearby. The car park has even had an extra level added to cope with increased demand.

FUTURE PLANS

There really isn't more that needs doing with the station, except perhaps the provision of more direct trains going to Birmingham and Oxford. At present most of the off peak services speed through the station. Maybe another car park will need to be built to cope with possible future demand.

Horwich Parkway (HW1)

Address: Off Arena Approach, Horwich, Greater Manchester BL6 6LB

Opened: July 2, 1999

Managed by: Northern Trains

Owned by: Transport for Greater Manchester

Train Operating Company using the station: Northern Trains

Destinations: Blackpool North, Hazel Grove, Manchester Airport, Manchester Piccadilly, Manchester Victoria, Preston

Frequency of off peak trains: 3 trains per hour to Preston, 2 of which continue to Blackpool North, 1 train per hour to Manchester Victoria, 1 train per hour to Manchester Airport, 1 train per hour to Hazel Grove

Number of platforms: 2

DfT Category: F1

Nearest towns: Horwich, Middlebrook

Nearby roads: A6, A6027, M61

Bus links: 505

Trivia: The station is actually owned by Transport for Greater Manchester, which put forward much of the finance needed to build the station.

No. 319382 arrives at Buckshaw Parkway station on August 13, 2019, with a train for Manchester Airport.

HISTORY

The railway line that Horwich Parkway is situated on runs from Manchester to Preston and was opened between 1838 and 1848. The town of Horwich grew from a village of almost 4000 inhabitants in 1881 to a town of 15,000 within 20 years. This was mainly due to the fact that the Lancashire and Yorkshire Railway built a large railway works in the town starting in 1884. Horwich had been connected to the main line from Blackrod in 1870 and this branch was used until 1983 when the Horwich Works closed down.

Much of the land where the Works stood has been redeveloped and is still being redeveloped today. In the late 1990s the Middlebrook retail, leisure and business complex was developed on a 200 acre site to the east of the works. Then in 1997 Bolton Wanderers FC relocated to the area from the centre of Bolton to the Reebok Stadium, as it was first called. The need for a railway station to cater for all these new developments led to the building of Horwich Parkway railway station which opened on July 2, 1999.

OVERVIEW

Horwich Parkway station on the Manchester to Preston route in the north west of England is one of those unusual parkway stations where a lot of its passenger traffic is incoming as opposed to outgoing. This is because of the nearby Bolton Wanderers Football Ground, the Middlebrook Shopping Centre and the Bolton Arena, a major sports venue, which are all within a short walk of the station. It's also virtually next to the M61 motorway, which connects Manchester to Preston and the M6. In addition, the town of Horwich (pop. 20,000) is just a couple of miles away.

So all in all it has a lot going for it. Passenger numbers have been up and down for the past five years, peaking in 2019/20 at 673,400. Factors like the electrification of the line, problems with the Northern Railways franchise and the pandemic have had an obvious effect on passenger

The station building at Horwich Parkway railway station.

numbers, but hopefully numbers will once again continue to rise.

The station itself has a modern station building with waiting area, toilets and ticket office which opened in 2007. The station has been brightened up by the various pictures on the platforms provided by pupils from a local school. There are long ramps on both platforms.

FUTURE PLANS

Since the electrification of the line from Manchester to Blackpool North in 2018-19, things have settled down both here and at other stations along the line, with services being more reliable and with newer trains with more capacity. The main aim of those running the station will be to get passenger numbers back to pre-COVID levels.

Liverpool South Parkway (LPY)

Address: Holly Farm Road, Garston, Merseyside L19 5NE

Opened: June 11, 2006

Managed by: Merseyrail

Train Operating Companies using the station: East Midlands Railway, London North Western Railway, Merseyrail, Northern Trains, Transport for Wales

Destinations: Birmingham New Street, Hunts Cross, Liverpool Lime Street, Manchester Airport, Manchester Oxford Road, Norwich, Nottingham, Southport, Wrexham General

Frequency of off peak trains: 4 trains per hour to Liverpool Central and Southport. 4 trains per hour to Manchester Oxford Road, one of which continues to Norwich. 2 trains per hour to Birmingham New Street. 1 train per hour to Chester. 7 trains per hour to Liverpool Lime Street

Number of platforms: 6

DfT category: B

Nearest towns: Liverpool, Runcorn, Widnes

Nearby roads: A561, B5171

Bus links: 80, 80A, 80E, 82, 82C, 82D, 86, 86A, 86D, 166, 167, 188, 201, 661, 786

Trivia: Liverpool Parkway is the largest of all the Parkway stations having six platforms.

The impressive frontage of Liverpool South Parkway railway station.

HISTORY

Liverpool South Parkway station was opened on June 11, 2006, on a site where originally two different railway lines passed near to each other at two separate stations. The first was the Cheshire Lines Committee (CLC) line which originally ran from Liverpool Central to Manchester Central via Warrington Central. This went under the second line, the Liverpool branch of the West Coast mainline running from Liverpool Lime Street to Crewe via Runcorn. This section, opened by the London and North Western Line in 1869, surpassed the original line from Liverpool to Crewe which went east as far as Warrington Bank Quay, where it joined with the West Coast Main line coming south from Preston.

The two stations on these lines were Garston on the Liverpool Central line and Allerton on the Liverpool Lime Street Line. Allerton was opened on February 15, 1864, while Garston was opened ten years later on April 1, 1874. Garston was the first to close in April 1972 when the whole line from Garston to Liverpool Central High Level was closed to make way for the Merseyrail Network being built. Trains from Manchester and Warrington Central were diverted onto the Lime Street line just east of Allerton station. Garston station reopened on January 3, 1978, being the southern terminus of the new Northern Line from Southport. However the line was extended one station to the east at Hunts Cross in 1983 where there are three platforms.

The idea for an interchange here had been first suggested back in the 1960s when plans for the Merseyrail network were starting to be made. The expansion of the former Speke Airport, which was renamed Liverpool John Lennon Airport in 2001, was the impetus for a rail and bus interchange at this site beginning to take shape. The need for a Park and Ride facility for passengers in the south Liverpool area was another motivating factor, as was the possibility of changing trains to travel between the Northern Line, the City Line and the West Coast mainline.

Work on the new Liverpool South Parkway station began in 2004, though Allerton station remained open until July 2005. Garston station didn't actually close until the day before the new station opened on June 11, 2006. The new platforms on the two lines were joined by an overhead walkway. The site of much of the new interchange station was once owned by Liverpool South Football Club. Whether the name of the station came from here is unclear.

OVERVIEW

Liverpool South Parkway is the biggest of the Parkway railway stations with six platforms, though in fact it is the amalgamation of two stations on two different lines that cross each other just to the east of the station. It was created mainly as the railhead for Liverpool John Lennon Airport which is less than three miles away.

Three routes serve the station—the West Coast mainline from Liverpool to London Euston via Crewe; the line from Manchester Piccadilly to Liverpool just to the east of the station, and the line from Southport to Hunts Cross which passes under these other lines and comes into the station on a lower part with two separate platforms. They are all joined by an overhead walkway with fine views of the tracks in both directions. There is a ticket office, shop and waiting area attached to this walkway.

The front of the station has a large, impressive, glass front with an area for bus stops. To the rear of the station is a 300 plus space car park with a taxi rank and drop off point. The station has been built to be as environmentally friendly as possible—with a 700,000 litre rainwater harvesting system which is recycled for the toilets. The roof uses recycled aluminium and all wood used in the construction of the station had to be certified as coming from a well-managed forest.

Passenger numbers have grown considerably since the station opened with almost 2.75 million people using it in 2018/19. Hopefully, numbers will eventually reach the three million mark once the effects of COVID-19 have died down. All the train operators that use Liverpool Lime Street also use Liverpool South Parkway apart from Avanti West Coast, due to the platforms being too short for its trains.

FUTURE PLANS

Although it was possible to get to London Euston directly from Liverpool South Parkway pre-COVID, this was only on London Northwestern trains, with a journey time of over four hours. As the platforms are not long enough to cope with 11 or 12 carriage trains, Avanti West Coast trains do not stop at the station. This is something that needs to be addressed as many people in the south Liverpool area going to London either have to go into Lime Street and out again, or change at Runcorn or Crewe.

In fact, when Liverpool Lime Street was shut for engineering works in the autumn of 2017 and the summer of 2018, West Coast mainline

**A Class 508 electric unit, No. 508134 departs from the
Northern Line platforms of Liverpool South Parkway
bound for Hunts Cross on November 10, 2018.**

trains did stop at the station with one of the platforms being temporarily extended. Perhaps if the platforms could be permanently extended then Avanti West Coast Trains could stop here, making a journey to London Euston in less than two hours possible.

With HS2 getting the go-ahead in February 2020, with an extension to Liverpool, having longer platforms to cope with the new trains will again need to be looked into.

Since 2019, Transport for Wales Rail has been operating trains through the station which go via the Halton Curve near Runcorn to Chester (and Wrexham in some cases). The possibility of a regular train service to the North Wales coast is now more likely, as are through trains via Shrewsbury to South Wales.

Luton Airport Parkway (LTN)

Address: Parkway Road, Luton, Bedfordshire, LU1 3JW

Opened: November 21, 1999

Managed by: Thameslink

Train Operating Companies using the station: East Midlands Railway, Thameslink

Destinations: Bedford, Brighton, Derby, East Grinstead, Gatwick Airport, Leeds, Littlehampton, London St Pancras International, Luton, Melton Mowbray, Nottingham, Orpington, Rainham (Kent), Sheffield

Number of platforms: 4

Frequency of off peak trains: 2 trains per hour to Luton, 4 trains an hour to Bedford, 1 train per hour to Nottingham, 1 train per hour to London St Pancras International, 2 trains per hour to Brighton, 2 trains per hour to Gatwick Airport, 2 trains per hour to Rainham (Kent)

DfT category: D

Nearest town: Luton

Nearby roads: A1081, M1

Bus links: 30, 44, 45, 366, 612 Dragonfly, Luton Airport Shuttle

Trivia: Luton Airport Parkway is by far the busiest of the Parkway stations in terms of passengers. Before COVID, more than four million people were using the station annually.

Reflecting the busy nature of Luton Airport Parkway station, a Class 700 electric unit, No. 700041 arrives with the 1548 departure for Brighton on March 23, 2019.

HISTORY

Luton Airport Parkway station was opened on November 21, 1999, being situated one mile south of Luton station on the Midland Main Line between London St Pancras and Sheffield. The line north from St Pancras to Bedford was opened in 1868, though the line further north had been opened several years before that, starting in 1839 with the line between Derby and Nottingham. Luton station was opened in the same year as the railway line and the town of Luton grew from a population of around 38,000 in 1900 to well over 200,000 a century later.

The airport was first opened in 1938 and was used as an RAF base during the Second World War. It became a civilian airport in 1952 and grew considerably in the 1960s and 1970s with the emerging package holiday boom. By the 1990s it was the fastest growing airport in the UK and during this time more than £30 million was invested in the airport's infrastructure. The Queen and Prince Philip opened a new terminal at the airport in November 1999, built at a cost of £40 million, but before that they opened a new station nearby: Luton Airport Parkway. The royal couple arrived on a Thameslink train from St Pancras and unveiled a plaque at the station.

OVERVIEW

Situated about two miles south of Luton town centre and about a mile away from Luton Airport, this is one of those parkway stations which benefits from passengers coming to it by train in larger numbers rather than by car. It still has a large car park though with more than 800 car parking spaces.

The station also has the advantage of being on the mainline between London St Pancras and Derby, Nottingham and Sheffield, though most of these services do not stop at the station. There are also the Thameslink electric trains from Bedford going south via the centre of London to Brighton or Rainham or Orpington. So the station is perhaps better connected to the south.

There are four long platforms situated high up above ground level and below these are two more levels before you get to the main entrance. The first floor has toilets and a café/newsagents, though it all seems quite small for such a busy and important station—after all Luton airport is the fourth busiest airport station in Britain. There is another exit to the north at street level which was opened in April 2013, though it is quite small.

FUTURE PLANS

At the time of writing Luton Airport Parkway does not have an express style train service between the airport and London such as

The massive station front of Luton Airport Parkway railway station.

those operated for Heathrow, Gatwick and Stansted Airports. With the change of operator on the East Midlands mainline in 2019, from East Midlands Trains to East Midlands Railway, it was hoped that the parent company, Abellio, would be introducing such a service. Once electrification is completed between Bedford and Corby, it is planned that a new express service will operate between London St Pancras and Luton Airport Parkway. This service was expected to be fully functional by December 2020 with trains every 30 minutes between the two stations but has been delayed to 2021. Eventually the aim was to have trains running every 15 minutes.

Also in the offing is a new £225 million rail link currently being built between Luton Airport Parkway station and the airport. This will be an automated guided people mover, which will give a journey time between the station and the airport of less than five minutes, considerably shorter than the current shuttle bus service it will replace. It is expected to be in place by 2021.

The impact of COVID on Luton Airport has been considerable with passenger numbers down by 80% for some months in 2020. This has had a knock on effect on Luton Airport Parkway with passenger numbers also considerably down. It will take some time before passenger numbers rise and whether they will regain the heights reached before the pandemic remains to be seen.

Oxford Parkway (OXP)

Address: Water Eaton Park & Ride, Oxford Road, Oxford OX2 8HA

Opened: October 25, 2015

Managed by: Chiltern Railways

Train Operating Company using the station: Chiltern Railways

Destinations: London Marylebone, Oxford

Number of platforms: 2

Frequency of off peak trains: 2 trains per hour to Oxford, 2 trains per hour to London Marylebone

Nearest towns: Bicester, Kidlington, Oxford

Nearby roads: A34, A40, M40

Bus links: 2, 2A, 2B, 3, 7 gold, 94, 250, 300, H4, N2, N7 gold, NS5 gold, S4 gold, S5 gold

Trivia: A local landmark, the large Water Eaton grain silo which had stood on the site of the station since the Second World War had to be demolished before work could proceed.

The distinctive looking entrance to Oxford Parkway railway station.

HISTORY

The line on which Oxford Parkway station is situated was originally part of the 'Varsity Line' running between the university cities of Oxford and Cambridge. The section between Oxford and Bletchley was first opened in 1851 as part of the Buckinghamshire Railway. When the Second World War began the Government started using the Varsity Line as a freight route to bypass London. After the war, traffic began to decline yet the Beeching Report of 1963 actually recommended keeping the line open. However, due to operating losses the line was again put forward for closure.

By 1968 the section of line between Bedford and Cambridge had been closed, along with the section between Oxford and Bicester being closed to passenger traffic. Thanks to a nearby army depot, Bicester remained open for freight trains and so did not close completely. In 1973 this section between Oxford and Bicester had a further setback when its double track was reduced to a single track.

Passenger services were restored in 1987, some 20 years after they had been withdrawn. In an initiative by Oxford County Council, Network South East started a new hourly service between Oxford and Bicester Town. Since then the setting up of Bicester Village retail centre has led to increased traffic on the line and in August 2008 Chiltern Railways announced Project Evergreen 3 — which would see a new service operating between Oxford and London Marylebone by 2012, including the building of a missing link at Bicester which would join the Chiltern Mainline to the Bicester Branch.

Chiltern Railways formally took over passenger operations on the line on May 22, 2011, and in February 2014 the line closed completely so work could begin on the new section. Also the track between Bicester and Oxford was upgraded, including the redoubling of the line and the building of a new station called 'Oxford Parkway' next to the Water Eaton Park and Ride facility.

The line reopened on October 25, 2015, connecting through trains from

London Marylebone to the newly opened Oxford Parkway station. It would be another year though until through trains ran all the way into Oxford station. The first through train from Oxford to London Marylebone ran on December 11, 2016, with a journey time of around an hour.

OVERVIEW

The whole line between Oxford and Bicester has been created to the most up to date standards with all the level crossings removed. Oxford Parkway is part of the regeneration of this line. Thanks to the building of the new curve at Bicester joining this, the old Varsity Line, with the Chiltern Mainline, it is now possible to get to London Marylebone from here in just over an hour.

A view looking down on a snowy Oxford Parkway railway station from the A34 with a London Marylebone train in the platforms on February 1, 2019.

Situated to the north of Oxford, near Kidlington, next to the A34 and by the Water Eaton Park & Ride, Oxford Parkway has gone from strength to strength since it first opened in 2015. Passenger numbers have almost quadrupled in the four years that it has been open, reaching the million mark in 2018/19. It is used not just by commuters going into Oxford or further afield to London, but also tourists visiting Oxford who can park all day for just £2, catch a train into Oxford and so avoid the hefty parking charges of the city car parks.

The station itself has two platforms, with just one shelter on the London bound platform. The main station building by the Oxford bound platform is coloured grey with blue glazed bricks. It contains toilets, a ticket office, a small café and waiting area. The very large car park with more than 800 spaces has been split into different sections and is right next to the station, unlike some other Parkway station car parks.

FUTURE PLANS

With the government giving the green light for the East-West route in January 2020, Oxford Parkway will serve several more destinations. Trains will go east to Bletchley and then either go north to Milton Keynes or east to Bedford and eventually to Cambridge. The resurrection of the line between Bicester and Bletchley is expected to be open by 2023.

Port Talbot Parkway (PTA)

(WELSH NAME — PARCFFORDD PORT TALBOT)

Address: Heilbronn Way, Port Talbot, West Glamorgan SA13 1UR

Opened: June 19, 1850, as Port Talbot. Changed its name to Port Talbot Parkway on December 3, 1984

Managed by: Transport for Wales

Train Operating Companies using the station: Great Western Railway, Transport for Wales

Destinations: Bristol Parkway, Cardiff Central, Carmarthen, Hereford, London Paddington, Manchester Piccadilly, Milford Haven, Newport, Pembroke Dock, Swansea

Frequency of off peak trains: 1 train per hour to London Paddington Manchester Piccadilly and Milford Haven, 2 trains per hour to Cardiff, 3 trains per hour to Swansea

Number of platforms: 2

DfT Category: D

Nearest town: Port Talbot

Nearby roads: A48, M4

Bus links: 87, 901, X1, X3

Trivia: Port Talbot was the only Parkway station in Wales for over 20 years until Ebbw Vale Parkway station opened in 2008.

A Class 800 Azuma train arrives at platform 2 of Port Talbot Parkway with the 14.40 service to London Paddington on July 14, 2019. The town centre is on the right of the picture.

HISTORY

Port Talbot Parkway station was originally opened as 'Port Talbot' station on June 19, 1850, when the line from Swansea to Chepstow was opened. Port Talbot at the time was a collection of several villages—namely Margam, Aberafan and Baglan—which grew into the conurbation that we know today. A set of docks on the river Afan had been opened as 'Port Talbot' in 1837, named for the Talbot family who owned land in the vicinity. The borough of Port Talbot did not actually come into being until 1921 when it was officially given that name.

With the coming of the M4 to the town in the 1960s (originally called the A48 (M) motorway), rail passengers were being lost in ever increasing numbers to the motor car. One idea was to re-brand Port Talbot station as a Parkway station instead and encourage motorists from the east Swansea and Neath areas to park their cars at Port Talbot and then take the train east from there, rather than use their local stations.

After all, Bodmin Road had been renamed Bodmin Parkway a year before in 1983. In addition, further down the line, Bristol Parkway had been a great success for over ten years by this point. So on December 3, 1984, Port Talbot became 'Port Talbot Parkway', even though it was very close to the town centre and not a new station. It did have the advantage of a large car park though, due to the demolition of an old goods shed next to the station. Over the years patronage has increased to around half a million users a year. In 2016 a new bridge crossing was installed at the station, which included a new ticket office, waiting room and lifts at a cost of £11 million.

OVERVIEW

Port Talbot Parkway is one those few Parkway stations which is situated in a town. This has caused some people to say that it is not really a 'proper' Parkway station, especially as it had its name changed in 1984. It has been used as a Park and Ride type station ever since though, the nearby M4 motorway giving it good road connections with Neath and Swansea.

**A view of the inside of the futuristic looking footbridge
at Port Talbot Parkway railway station.**

The station is unusual, not only for its 'space age' design but also for the fact that it is the only Parkway station to have a single island platform. This has meant that to comply with the requirements of the Disability Discrimination Act for accessibility, lifts are necessary to access the island platform.

Between 2014 and 2016 the station was rebuilt at a cost of £11 million as part of the Wales Station Improvement Scheme. A new 400 tonne footbridge with lifts was put into place with a new ticket office, toilets and disabled access, as well as an updated waiting room. Inside it could be said that it looks like a scene from a *Stars Wars* movie with grey walls and no windows at the sides. Outside, some say that the footbridge resembles an origami puzzle with all its triangular parts! The car park was also enlarged from 111 spaces to just under 150. Passenger numbers have grown steadily over the past few years with 545,000 visitors using the station in 2019/20.

FUTURE PLANS

While the line is not going to be electrified between Cardiff and Swansea in the near future, Port Talbot Parkway does have a wide choice of destinations to travel including Cardiff, London, Manchester, Bristol and Hereford in the east; and Swansea, Pembroke and Milford Haven in the west. There are plans for the Swanline service which currently operates between Swansea and Cardiff every two hours to be terminated at Port Talbot Parkway and run every hour instead.

There is also the possibility of a 'West Wales Parkway' station being built to the north of Swansea, which could eat into the number of passengers currently using Port Talbot Parkway, especially if it saves them having to drive as far.

Southampton Airport Parkway (SOA)

Address: Wide Lane, Southampton, Hampshire SO18 2HW

Opened: October 30, 1929, as Atlantic Park Hostel Halt, then closed. Reopened on April 1, 1966, as Southampton Airport. Renamed Southampton Parkway for Southampton (Eastleigh) Airport on September 29, 1986. Renamed again to Southampton Airport (Parkway) on May 29, 1994.

Managed by: South Western Railway

Train Operating Companies using the station: Cross Country, Great Western Railway, Southern, South Western Railway

Destinations: Birmingham New Street, Bournemouth, Brighton, London Waterloo, Manchester Piccadilly, Portsmouth Harbour, Romsey, Salisbury, Southampton Central, Weymouth, Winchester, York

Frequency of off peak trains: 3 trains per hour to London Waterloo, 1 train per hour to Romsey via Chandlers Ford, 1 train per hour to Salisbury via Southampton, 4 trains per hour to Bournemouth, 3 trains per hour to Poole, 2 trains per hour to Weymouth, 1 train per hour to Manchester Piccadilly

Number of platforms: 2

DfT category: C1

Nearest towns: Eastleigh, Southampton

Nearby roads: A335, M27, M3

Bus links: M34, U1C, U1E, X4, X21

Trivia: Southampton Airport Parkway railway station is the only one of the Parkway railway stations to have the Parkway name in brackets, as shown on its station signs.

The main station entrance to Southampton Airport Parkway railway station.

HISTORY

The line on which Southampton Parkway stands runs from London Waterloo to Weymouth and was electrified using the 750 V DC third rail system as far as Bournemouth in 1967 and then onto Weymouth in 1988.

This section of track was opened in 1839 and became part of the 'South Western Main Line'.

Southampton Municipal Airport opened next to the line south of Eastleigh station in 1932 after Southampton Corporation purchased the site from the Atlantic Park Hostel Company, which had previously owned the site. Meanwhile, the airport continued to grow and became an RAF station before the Second World War began, eventually becoming a Royal Navy training base. After the war it developed as an airfield once more. It was home to a cross-channel car ferry air service and various factories were built around its perimeter.

In 1959 the airport was bought by J N 'Nat' Somers, a racing pilot who developed the site further—including the construction of a concrete runway which opened in 1963. He also managed to persuade British Railways to build a new station next to the airport called 'Southampton Airport', which opened in 1966. The airport expanded over the next 50 years to become the 18th busiest airport in the UK, being taken over by Heathrow Airport Holdings (formerly BAA) during the 1990s and then its present owners AGS Airports in 2014.

The railway station had its name changed to Southampton Parkway station in 1986, which tied in with the opening of the M27 just to the south of the station in 1983. However, with the growth of Southampton Airport another change of name was put forward which combined both the names 'Airport' and 'Parkway' in its title. So in 1994 it became 'Southampton Airport (Parkway)'. It was believed that brackets were used to indicate that this is the station that was formerly called 'Parkway'. To this day the brackets are still in use on the station platform name boards and above the main entrance, though timetable and electronic information boards do not have the brackets.

OVERVIEW

Southampton Airport Parkway has gone from strength to strength over the years, with 1.7 million passengers using it in 2018/19. People tend to come to the station in large numbers by train, primarily to go to the airport, rather than using it as a Park and Ride. There are more than 900 parking spaces in two car parks, both virtually next to the station, with airport passengers leaving their cars here while they go on holiday.

Having the airport terminal right next to the station is a key advantage — the slogan, 'Less than 100 paces from station to terminal' was used in the airport's advertising at one time. It is also near junction 5 of the M27, which in turn is connected to the M3 and London. Virtually all the trains passing through the station stop here, which means there

Looking down platform 2 of Southampton Airport Parkway towards Southampton. Note the open shelters on the platforms.

are a wide variety of destinations, both local and national. There were 10 at the last count.

The main entrance is on the west side of the station, while the east side has another entrance/exit which leads straight into Southampton Airport terminal; hence the name. The platforms are very long to cater for 12-car trains and there is a main building on the west side which has a ticket office, café, shop and waiting area.

There are no bus type shelters on either platform; instead there are canopies on both sides, the longer one being on the airport side. There is a covered staircase and lifts at the north end of the station, as well as an older footbridge at the south end of the station.

FUTURE PLANS

The future of the station is linked to the future of Southampton Airport, which has gradually grown over the past 20 years. If the airport continues to expand, so will the station. Unlike some of the other British Airports, most of its flights tend to be within the UK or to the nearer parts of Europe. In spite of COVID, British Airways is expected to start operating new flights to various European destinations in 2021, which should bring more passengers to the station.

Stratford-Upon-Avon Parkway (STY)

Address: Bishopton Lane, Stratford-upon-Avon, Warwickshire CV37 9QY

Opened: May 19, 2013

Managed by: West Midlands Trains

Train Operating Companies using the station: Chiltern Railways, West Midlands Trains

Destinations: Birmingham Snow Hill, Kidderminster, Leamington Spa, London Marylebone, Stourbridge Junction, Stratford-upon-Avon, Warwick, Worcester Foregate Street, Worcester Shrub Hill

Frequency of off peak trains: 2 trains per hour to Stourbridge Junction via Birmingham Snow Hill, 2 trains per hour to Stratford-upon-Avon, 1 train per two hours to Leamington Spa or London Marylebone

Number of platforms: 2

Nearest town: Stratford-upon-Avon

Nearby roads: A46, A3400, M40

Bus links: Park and Ride Bus into Stratford-upon-Avon town centre only

Trivia: This Parkway station is one of only three Parkway stations not to have a station building.

Stratford-upon-Avon Parkway station looking north along platform 1 with identical shelters on each platform.

HISTORY

Stratford-upon-Avon Parkway station lies on the lines from Birmingham Moor Street to Stratford-upon-Avon via Shirley, known as the 'North Warwickshire Line', and on the branch line from Hatton on the Chiltern main line. This branch line was opened by the Stratford on Avon Railway in 1860 which connected it with the Great Western mainline from London Paddington to Birmingham Snow Hill. The direct line north to Birmingham didn't open to passengers until July 1908. It survived various attempts to close it down, first in the 1960s during the Beeching Cuts era and then in 1984, though the line beyond Stratford-upon-Avon to Cheltenham was closed in 1976.

Stratford-upon-Avon, being a popular tourist destination with its links to William Shakespeare, has had traffic congestion for many years; it was therefore decided to open a Parkway railway station by the existing Bishopton Park and Ride facility on the northern outskirts of the town, just off the A46 trunk road.

The idea was that motorists would be able to catch a train (or bus) into the centre of the town and so ease congestion. Work on the station started on October 17, 2012, and was completed seven months ahead of schedule with the station opening to passengers on May 19, 2013.

OVERVIEW

Stratford-upon-Avon Parkway station is one of the newest Parkway railway stations, having opened in May 2013 at a cost of over £8 million. It is situated just half a mile north of Stratford-upon-Avon railway station next to the A46 trunk road and seven miles from junction 15 of the M40. It is designed to keep tourist traffic out of Stratford-upon-Avon, as well as being a useful station for commuters wishing to catch trains into Birmingham or to nearby Warwick and Leamington Spa.

While some passengers might use Stratford-upon-Avon Parkway as a way of commuting into Birmingham to the north, the majority of the passengers using it are tourists visiting Stratford-upon-Avon.

A Class 165 *Networker* diesel unit, No. 165024 comes into
Stratford-upon-Avon Parkway station with a stopping
service to Leamington Spa on February 2, 2019.

Stratford-upon-Avon is not large (pop. 27,000) but receives around three
million tourists each year.

The station being right next to Stratford-upon-Avon's Park and Ride
facility can cause problems in that some tourists will take a Park and Ride
bus into Stratford-upon-Avon as opposed to the train. The station does
have trains running right through the evening until 11.30pm (Monday to
Saturday) however, whereas the Park and Ride buses do not operate after
7pm on weekdays and not at all on a Sunday. So the train beats the bus
here, especially if passengers want to go to the theatre during the week.

Passenger numbers have been encouraging with year on year growth, apart from 2016/17 when the number fell by a couple of thousand. The 100,000 mark was topped in 2019, which is encouraging, though COVID has reduced passenger numbers in 2020. The car park has almost 300 spaces and station facilities include ramps and steps over the footbridge. There are two identical shelters on each platform—in fact the platforms look like mirror images of each other as regards space and design. There is no station building at the time of writing; just a ticket machine on the car park side.

FUTURE PLANS

A station building with a ticket office and toilets at least would be a welcome addition, making it more passenger friendly. Also Chiltern Railways did run more direct trains to London Marylebone a few years ago and these are not as frequent. Perhaps more of these would benefit the station, especially in the summer months.

Sutton Parkway (SPK)

Address: Low Moor Road, Sutton-in-Ashfield, Nottinghamshire NG17 5LG

Opened: October 20, 1995

Managed by: East Midlands Railway

Train Operating Company using the station: East Midlands Railway

Destinations: Mansfield Woodhouse, Norwich, Nottingham, Worksop

Frequency of off peak trains: 2 trains per hour to Nottingham, 2 trains per hour to Mansfield Woodhouse, one of which continues to Worksop

Number of platforms: 2

DfT category: F1

Nearest town: Sutton-in-Ashfield

Nearby roads: A38, B6021, M1

Bus links: 3C, The Black Cat

Trivia: The road to the north of the station is called Penny Emma Lane. This was the nickname of the train which used to take passengers from Sutton-in-Ashfield to the main line at Sutton Junction. The cost of the fare was one penny and 'Emma' comes from the initials of the Midland Railway, which ran the trains—MR, which could be seen on the side of the locomotives.

The view north over Sutton Parkway railway station in Nottinghamshire.

HISTORY

Sutton Parkway station lies on the Robin Hood Line which runs from Nottingham to Worksop via Mansfield. It was first opened by the Mansfield and Pixton Railway, before being taken over by the Midland Railway in the 1840s. Sutton-in-Ashfield is a few miles west of this line and it wasn't until 1917 that it got its own station. This was linked with the Midland Railway line with a branch from Sutton Junction station, which was about half a mile north of the present Sutton Parkway station. In fact the local council ward is still known as Sutton Junction.

Sutton-in-Ashfield station closed to timetabled passenger and goods traffic in 1956, while Sutton Junction station closed in 1964, along with Mansfield. The latter location eventually became known as 'the largest town in Britain without a railway station'. It would be another 30 years before Mansfield got its station back.

The line through Mansfield reopened in 1995 using parts of the original route and some existing freight lines. It was given the name 'The Robin Hood Line' and in addition to Mansfield reopening, Mansfield Woodhouse also reopened, as well as a new station being created, 'Sutton Parkway', not far from the old Sutton Junction station.

The cost of the station was just £650,000, paid for by Ashfield District Council. The line north of Mansfield Woodhouse through to Worksop opened in 1998.

OVERVIEW

Sutton Parkway station is one of the most basic Parkway stations on the railway network. It has two platforms with just the bus stop type waiting shelters on each platform. There are no station facilities such as a waiting room, toilets or a ticket office. It is permanently unmanned with no ticket gates, though there are help points and ticket machines on each platform.

There are also the older type electronic display screens on each platform. It has been built according to modern accessibility standards with ramps to each platform. Noticeable on the floor tiles of each platform are the Robin Hood Line logos of two arrows intertwined. There are two small car parks on either side of the station with spaces for about 100 cars in total which were free at the time of writing. There are also 20 bicycle storage spaces.

It was built to serve Sutton-in-Ashfield (pop. 46,000) two miles away, though you do get the impression of remoteness. It is a mixture of fields and industrial units in the vicinity of the station, but if you do go a little further afield there is some housing hidden away. The West Nottinghamshire College Construction Centre Station Park is also nearby. The station's remoteness is not helped by the fact that there isn't a taxi rank

Class 156 diesel unit, No. 156401 on a service to Mansfield Woodhouse
leaving Sutton Parkway railway station on April 10, 2019.

at the station and only an hourly bus service between the station and the town. This remoteness can be a problem, as demonstrated in September 2019 when 10 cars were vandalised in one of the station car parks.

On the bright side, passenger numbers using the station have been steadily climbing over the past few years, with just under 200,000 recorded for the period 2019/20. With a train every half hour to both Nottingham and Mansfield, numbers post-COVID should start to rise again. A more frequent bus service between the town and the station would help.

FUTURE PLANS

Although there are no definite plans for Sutton Parkway, perhaps a change of name might be helpful. It would do no harm to rename Sutton Parkway as Sutton-in-Ashfield Parkway since that is the town that it serves. In fact, it was originally going to be called Sutton-in-Ashfield in the planning stages. It would certainly help to put Sutton-in-Ashfield on the map more. When they think of Sutton, most people think of Sutton in south London. Some people would even argue that Sutton Parkway is too close a name to Sutton Park, another station in south London. So a clearer, more precise name could help the station's profile.

Tame Bridge Parkway (TAB)

Address: Walsall Road, Friar Park, Wednesbury, West Midlands WS10 0LD

Opened: June 4, 1990

Managed by: West Midlands Trains and London Northwestern Railway

Train Operating Company using the station: West Midlands Trains

Destinations: Birmingham International, Birmingham New Street, Northampton, Rugeley Trent Valley, Walsall, Wolverhampton

Frequency of off peak trains: 4 trains per hour to Birmingham New Street, 2 of which continue to Wolverhampton and to Birmingham International, 4 trains per hour to Walsall, 2 of which continue to Rugeley Trent Valley

Number of platforms: 2

DfT category: E

Nearest towns: Birmingham, West Bromwich, Walsall

Nearby roads: A4031, M5, M6

Bus links: 4, 4H, 4M, 41, 45

Trivia: The station isn't actually situated in a place called Tame Bridge. Instead it gets its name from the River Tame which runs close to the station.

The station building at Tame Bridge Parkway railway station.

HISTORY

Tame Bridge Parkway station was opened by British Rail on June 4, 1990, at a cost of £600,000. It is situated on the line from Birmingham New Street to Walsall and Rugeley. This stretch of line actually opened in 1837 as the Grand Junction Railway, which ran from Birmingham to north Wolverhampton via Perry Barr and then on to Stafford, Crewe and Warrington. There was no station here previously, with the nearest station being Bescot Bridge (now called Bescot Stadium) in Walsall, about a mile to the north. The area between the two stations is now part of the large Bescot Yard, which for many years has been the main centre for handling the various freight movements in the West Midlands area.

Tame Bridge Parkway was chosen as a Parkway station mainly due to its location near to where the M5 and M6 motorways diverge. In fact it is only half a mile away from Junction 8 of the M6, though there is no motorway access from the A4031 which runs past the station. Instead the nearest access to the M6 is at junction 9 which is nearer to Bescot Stadium station, though there is little land there for a car park.

At the time of its construction the line between Birmingham Snow Hill and Wolverhampton Low Level had been closed to passengers since 1972. It would be another nine years before this line was opened as a tram route, so it was felt a new station which served the communities of West Bromwich and Wednesbury should be built.

The station is situated next to the A4031 dual carriageway which links Walsall in the north with West Bromwich in the south.

OVERVIEW

This well-patronised station is situated on the borders of Birmingham and Walsall on the line from Birmingham New Street to Walsall. In fact it is probably the only Parkway station sited within a large conurbation apart from Bristol Parkway. It had almost 700,000 passengers in 2018/19, reflecting an upward growth over the past few years. It helps that Birmingham New Street is only 15 minutes away by the fastest trains.

Although the M5 and M6 motorways run quite close to the station, there is no motorway access here, so there is a loss of potential custom.

As it was built into a cutting, the station has steps and a slope leading to both platforms. It is also at the south end of Bescot Yard, a major freight distribution railhead. It once had a through express service to London Marylebone on the Wrexham & Shropshire Open Access service which used Tame Bridge Parkway as its station stop for Birmingham. The company ceased trading in 2011 after almost three years of losses.

Prior to COVID there were through trains to London, but these took almost three hours to reach Euston and stopped at just about every

Looking north towards Bescot Yard at Tame Bridge Parkway railway station.

station it is possible to stop at between Birmingham and London. It was much quicker to change at Birmingham New Street.

The main car park to the north of the station was free at the time of writing and there are plenty of bike racks by the ticket office which is on the north side of the station.

FUTURE PLANS

Although the station is served by a wide choice of destinations it still would benefit from a direct service to Wolverhampton going north. You can get a train direct to Wolverhampton, but it goes via Birmingham and takes about an hour. With a northbound service it would take around 15 minutes — which would be more attractive to passengers. The service was stopped in 2008 due to poor patronage, but with the right publicity it could be a useful and popular service for local people.

Tiverton Parkway (TVP)

Address: Station Road, Sampford Peverell, Devon EX16 7EH

Opened: May 12, 1986

Managed by: Great Western Railway

Train Operating Companies using the station: Cross Country, Great Western Railway

Destinations: Aberdeen, Birmingham New Street, Bristol Temple Meads, Edinburgh, Exeter St Davids, Leeds, London Paddington, Newcastle, Paignton, Penzance, Plymouth

Frequency of off peak trains: 1 train per hour to London Paddington, 2 trains to per hour to Plymouth, 1 train per two hours to Manchester Piccadilly

Number of platforms: 2

DfT category: D

Nearest town: Tiverton

Nearby roads: A361, M5

Bus links: 1, 1C

Trivia: As the station is very close to the M5 motorway, the car park is often used as a coach park for when passengers have to leave a train at the station and then get a coach for the rest of their journey. When the line between Exeter and Plymouth was closed due to sea wall damage at Dawlish in 2014, an extra temporary coach park was built by the station to cope with the large number of vehicles using it.

A Cross Country HST train bound for Penzance arrives at Tiverton Parkway railway station on April 5, 2019.

HISTORY

Tiverton Parkway station lies on the site of the former railway station of Sampford Peverell, which opened in July 1928. The line through the station was opened on May 1, 1844, by the Bristol and Exeter Railway as a broad gauge track and was eventually taken over by the Great Western Railway and became part of the Bristol to Exeter main line. A branch line to Tiverton was opened two miles further south in 1848 with a station called Tiverton Junction linking it to the main line.

Sampford Railway station was closed on October 5, 1964, though Tiverton Junction remained open until Tiverton Parkway opened in 1986, though the branch to Tiverton also closed to passengers in 1964 and to freight three years later.

Tiverton Parkway was designed both as a railhead for Tiverton (pop. 38,000), six miles to the west and in response to the nearby M5 motorway which could be accessed at Junction 27. It was also by the A361 trunk road, which carries traffic across north Devon from Barnstaple and other nearby towns to the M5 motorway.

The station was opened by the then Minister of Transport, David Mitchell, on May 11, 1986. Its £730,000 cost was mainly paid for by British Railways, with other contributions coming from Devon County Council and the Mid-Devon District Council.

OVERVIEW

Although Tiverton Parkway is now over 30 years old, the station building still looks quite modern. With over half a million passengers using the station in 2019/20 it could be argued that it is a good example of a Parkway station that is working well. Certainly the station is attractive for car users, being right next to the M5 and having a car park with 400 plus spaces. It also has storage for 40 bicycles, being on the National Cycle Route 3 (Bristol to Land's End).

There is a pleasant waiting area, café and ticket office in the main building, with ramps to the footbridge across the tracks. A wide choice of

**The station building on the London bound platform
at Tiverton Parkway railway station.**

possible destinations is available including London, Edinburgh, Newcastle and Aberdeen.

FUTURE PLANS

While there are no definite plans to change anything to do with the station at present, it is interesting to see that with the introduction of the bi-mode Class 800 trains, some trains to and from London are now going via Bristol and Bristol Parkway, offering an alternative journey to the capital for passengers.

Warwick Parkway (WRP)

Address: Old Budbrooke Road, near Warwick, Warwickshire CV35 8RH
Opened: October 25, 2000
Managed by: Chiltern Railways
Train Operating Companies using the station: Chiltern Railways, West Midlands Trains
Destinations: Banbury, Birmingham Moor Street, Birmingham Snow Hill, Kidderminster, London Marylebone, Stourbridge Junction
Frequency of off peak trains: 2 trains per hour to Birmingham Moor Street, 2 trains an hour to London Marylebone
Number of platforms: 2
DfT category: D
Nearest towns: Coventry, Leamington Spa, Warwick
Nearby roads: A46, A4177, M40
Bus links: 16, X17
Trivia: Warwick Parkway station is owned and managed by Chiltern Railways unlike many other stations which are owned by Network Rail.

The newly refurbished Warwick Parkway station building in October 2019.

HISTORY

Warwick Parkway was opened on October 25, 2000, on the London Marylebone to Birmingham Snow Hill line. The line had been opened in 1854 by the Great Western Railway on the route from London Paddington to Birkenhead via Birmingham Snow Hill. This flourished well into the 20th century, but with the electrification of the West Coast main line in the 1960s the line began to decline. The long distance Paddington to Birkenhead expresses were withdrawn in 1967 as part of 'The Reshaping of British Railways' and Birmingham Snow Hill was closed altogether in 1972, with Birmingham Moor Street becoming the northern terminus for the line.

Through trains between Birmingham and London also ceased for a time in the 1980s with Banbury being the limit for trains going south or north from London. Snow Hill station reopened in 1986, with trains eventually going through to Stourbridge and Kidderminster by the mid 1990s.

The opening of the M40 north from Oxford to Birmingham was the main impetus for the line growing once more. The motorway led to more urban development in the towns by the motorway including Banbury, Leamington and Warwick, which in turn led to more patronage of the railway.

With privatisation in the 1990s and Chiltern Railways taking over the line there was more money for investment and new, faster trains were brought in. As a result of increasing passenger numbers at Warwick and Leamington Spa, the new Warwick Parkway station was opened in 2000 with better road connections and plenty of parking space. It was built next to the A46 trunk road and near to Junction 7 of the M40; perfect for drawing in motorists who wished to commute into Birmingham or even down to London.

OVERVIEW

Warwick Parkway is only a mile west of Warwick station but nevertheless attracts passengers from the town since parking there is restricted.

The London bound platform at Warwick Parkway with the distinctive looking lift shaft and multi-storey car park beyond that.

It also serves the nearby villages of Budbrooke and Hampton Magna and other towns including Stratford-upon-Avon, Redditch, Coventry and even Bromsgrove. This is because it has a frequent service both into Birmingham (20 minutes) and London Marylebone (less than one hour 30 minutes in most cases).

The station building underwent a refurbishment in 2018-2019 and now has a waiting area with a small cafe plus a ticket office which is unusual as it is completely open with no glass frontage.

The platforms are higher up from the station building, being reached by stairs or lifts. These are similar to those at Coleshill Parkway, each having the square flat roof. On the south side of the station can be seen

106

farms and fields giving the impression of a country station. Yet on the opposite side is a multi-storey car park built in 2012, bringing the number of parking spaces at the station to just over 700.

FUTURE PLANS

The 2018-19 refurbishment saw facilities for passengers awaiting trains improved considerably. The only improvement to make now would be a faster train service to London. The coming of HS2 may affect passenger numbers in the future, but in 2018/19 almost 700,000 passengers were using the station. Since COVID, numbers have understandably decreased. Whether the commuters who once used this station will continue to work from home remains to be seen.

Whittlesford Parkway (WLF)

Address: Station Road, Whittlesford, Cambridgeshire CB22 4NL

Opened: July 30, 1845, as Whittlesford. Renamed 'Whittlesford Parkway' in May 2007

Managed by: Greater Anglia

Train Operating Company using the station: Great Anglia

Destinations: Cambridge, Cambridge North, Kings Lynn, London Liverpool Street, Norwich, Stansted Airport

Frequency of off peak trains: 2 trains per hour to London Liverpool Street, 1 train per hour to Stansted Airport, 2 trains per hour to Cambridge North, 1 train per hour to Norwich

Number of platforms: 2

DfT Category: E

Nearest towns: Cambridge, Duxford, Haverhill, Newmarket

Nearby roads: A505, M11

Bus links: 7

Trivia: Whittlesford is the only Parkway railway station to be sited to the east of the Greenwich Meridian. It also has the oldest station building still in use of all the Parkway stations, dating from 1890.

A view of Whittlesford Parkway railway station looking south with a hotel on the left and the Victorian station building on the right.

HISTORY

The original Whittlesford railway station was opened on July 30, 1845, on the same day as the line north from Bishops Stortford to Cambridge and Norwich was opened by the Eastern Counties Railway. The line eventually became the main West Anglia Line from London Liverpool Street to Cambridge. Originally there was a level crossing for the main road next to the station, but it wasn't until November 1960 that an over bridge was opened to cope with increased motor traffic using the A505.

The line was electrified through the station to Cambridge in 1987. A new footbridge had to be built to cope with the new electric wires, while the former foot bridge found a new home at the Colne Valley railway. In May 2007 the station name was changed from Whittlesford to Whittlesford Parkway. This was seen as an attempt by the then Train Operating Company to draw passengers away from driving into Cambridge and use Whittlesford Parkway instead for London services. Also many passengers from Haverhill to the east and Newmarket to the north were also using the station. An extra car park was then built on the east side of the station with approximately 200 spaces.

OVERVIEW

Whittlesford Parkway is a pleasant country station in the village of Whittlesford about ten miles south of Cambridge. It is well served though, with regular trains to London Liverpool Street, Cambridge, Norwich and Stansted Airport. There are three car parks nearby, the smallest being the original car park right next to the station building with about ten spaces. Then there is a long strip of car parking spaces next to the northbound railway line with about 20 spaces. Finally, there is a much larger car park hidden from view to the north of the station beyond the Holiday Inn hotel with about 300 spaces.

The village of Whittlesford is on the west side of the station, just a short walk away. The medieval building of Duxford Chapel is next to the station on the east side. At the south end of the platforms the A505

**A different view of the station building at
Whittlesford Parkway railway station.**

goes over the station. It runs to the south of Cambridge and joins up with the M11 about five minutes drive away, which helps make this an ideal Parkway station for motorists.

FUTURE PLANS

While there are no set plans for the future, the station does not have any lifts or a ramp, so disabled passengers wishing to cross platforms have to walk a long way round the station and cross the tracks on the A505 bridge. Perhaps a ramp could be built to resolve this problem.

Worcestershire Parkway (WOP)

Address: Whittington Road, Norton, Worcestershire WR7 4RD

Opened: February 23, 2020

Managed by: Great Western Railway

Train Operating Companies using the station: Cross Country, Great Western Railway

Destinations: Birmingham New Street, Cardiff Central, Gloucester, Great Malvern, Hereford, Leicester, London Paddington, Nottingham, Worcester Foregate Street, Worcester Shrub Hill

Frequency of off peak trains: 1 train per hour to Birmingham, London Paddington, Cardiff and Worcester Shrub Hill

Number of platforms: 3

Nearest towns: Bromsgrove, Evesham, Worcester

Nearby roads: B4084, A44, M5

Bus links: X50

Trivia: It is the only Parkway station on two levels where the Cotswold line passes over the Birmingham to Bristol mainline.

The main entrance to the newly-opened Worcestershire Parkway railway station taken in February 2020.

HISTORY

Worcestershire Parkway is situated where two railway lines cross. The first is the mainline from Birmingham to Bristol. This was opened by the Birmingham to Gloucester Railway in 1840, though for some reason its route bypassed Worcester. The second line is the Cotswold Line running from Oxford to Worcester. This was originally called the Oxford, Worcester & Wolverhampton and was formed in 1844, but the first trains didn't run until 1850, when a four mile stretch linking Worcester to the Birmingham to Bristol mainline was built.

The line from Worcester to Evesham was opened to rail traffic in 1853, crossing over the first line near to Abbots Wood Junction. Although a railway station was opened here in 1850, it only lasted five years before closing.

Over the years there were suggestions for siting a railway station here as an interchange between the two lines. For example, in 1977 Worcestershire County Council conducted a survey to ask whether local people would use a station there. Then in the early 2000s, plans were drawn up for a Park and Ride station.

However, it wasn't until 2015 that planning permission for the station was given, with work due to start in 2016. Work finally started in 2018 with a completion date given of early 2019 but problems with the embankment and drainage caused delays. An opening date of December 18, 2019, was given and widely reported in the media but even this was put back until early 2020 due to several parts of the station not being 'signed off'. It finally opened on February 23, 2020.

OVERVIEW

When Worcestershire Parkway station finally opened it became the first new railway station in Worcestershire for over 100 years. Being the newest Parkway station on Britain's railway network, it is also the most up to date in terms of facilities. There is a 500-space car park including electric car charging points, a drop off/pick up area, a taxi rank and

**A view looking south along the Bristol to Birmingham Line
at Worcestershire Parkway railway station with the glass
panelled overbridge and the Cotswold Line beyond that.**

a bus interchange. The station itself is fully accessible with lifts, café, toilets and a ticket office. There are currently three platforms; one on the Paddington to Worcester line and two on the Bristol to Birmingham line. The local wildlife have also been catered for with a wildlife corridor and a nature reserve. Part of the station building even has a 'living roof' to encourage wildlife.

The station is intended to attract customers not only from nearby Worcester, but also the various villages in the area. With this in mind there are direct trains to Oxford, London Paddington, Birmingham New Street, Nottingham, Cheltenham and Gloucester. In fact the Birmingham New Street trains take about 30 minutes from Worcestershire Parkway as opposed to 45 minutes from Worcester Shrub Hill.

FUTURE PLANS

Although it is early days, the obvious development for Worcestershire Parkway would be for train services going south to Bristol and the South West to stop at the station. Another possible future development is for trains to run from Kidderminster south to Worcester and then on to the Cotswold line south to London.

Finally, the line between Evesham and Norton Junction to the west of the station is single track. The redoubling of this section should be a priority and then a fourth platform could be added to the station and more frequent trains along this stretch of line would be guaranteed.

Unfortunately, the station opened just as the Coronavirus pandemic was starting in Britain, so it would be too early to say whether the station has attracted the predicted numbers of passengers or not.

CHAPTER 5

Former Parkway stations

Over the years there have been several Parkway stations opened which, for various reasons, dropped the Parkway suffix after a while. Here is a list of them in date order.

Alfreton and Mansfield Parkway was the second Parkway station to be built and was opened on May 7, 1973, as mentioned earlier in this book. Its name was changed to 'Alfreton' in 1995 on the reopening of Mansfield station on the Robin Hood Line. Alfreton however, still had plenty of passengers pre-COVID with more than 300,000 passing through the station in 2019/20.

Lostock Parkway near Bolton had originally opened in August 1852 as 'Lostock Junction'. This closed in November 1966 as part of the Beeching cuts. It was reopened on May 16, 1988, as Lostock Parkway, but in 1989 the station became plain 'Lostock'. Nevertheless, the information display boards at stations in and around Greater Manchester were still showing trains as stopping at 'Lostock Parkway' well into the 21st century!

Sandwell & Dudley Parkway in the West Midlands replaced the former Oldbury station and was opened on May 16, 1983. Situated on the mainline between Birmingham New Street and Wolverhampton it eventually lost its Parkway suffix.

A station sign showing 'Worle Parkway' at Worle railway station.

Worle Parkway station near Weston-super-Mare in Somerset, on the mainline from Bristol to the South West was opened in September 1990 by British Rail as 'Worle'. Around 2011-13 the name of the station became 'Worle Parkway' when an extra car park was built, as reflected in street signage and the signs outside the station. The station name in recent years has returned to plain 'Worle'.

CHAPTER 6

Parkway station failures

The phenomenon of Parkway stations seems to be well established after nearly 50 years with 22 in existence in 2020 with several more in the pipeline. The best laid plans can fall apart, however. There are several instances of proposed parkway stations that came to nothing. Here are some of them.

FLETTON PARKWAY

This station would have been on the Peterborough to Huntingdon stretch of the East Coast mainline on the southern edge of Peterborough. Proposed during the days of Railtrack, it was intended to serve the community of Hampton and a new development that would be called 'Fletton'. Problems with the developers meant that it never got going. Instead, in recent years, more platforms have been added at Peterborough station to cater for the increasing number of passengers and trains using the station.

GLOUCESTERSHIRE PARKWAY

When Gloucester railway station was built in the 1800s it was to the west of the mainline from Birmingham to Bristol which was built afterwards. Consequently it has missed out on express trains calling at the station. In the early 2000s proposals were put forward for this station to be built by the A40 at Elmbridge Court, 1½ miles east of Gloucester. Plans were put forward in 2006, but were dismissed by the Department for Transport a year later.

HINKSEY PARKWAY

This was a proposed Parkway station at Hinksey to the south west of Oxford, near the A34 western bypass. The problem was that the railway track here was prone to flooding and so the financial risk was deemed to be too great. Remedial work to prevent flooding took place in 2016, which involved raising the track level by 2ft. In the end Oxford Parkway was built to the north of the city, opening in 2015.

IVER PARKWAY

This would have been the perfect Parkway station, being situated next to the M4 and M25 to the west of London. Iver Parkway station would have been situated on the Great Western mainline a few miles to the east of Slough. Unfortunately, there were no accessible junctions of the M4 or M25 within easy reach, and so it was a non-starter.

MILTON PARKWAY

This station was to have been built to the north of Cambridge on the Cambridge to Ely line by the A14. Instead a station serving the north of Cambridge, called Cambridge North, opened in 2017.

- Other Parkway stations that never came to fruition include: Barnstaple Parkway, Patcham Parkway, Plymouth Parkway, Springfield Parkway, West Yorkshire Parkway.

CHAPTER 7

Future Parkway stations

There are several more Parkway stations which might be opened in the coming years, subject to the relevant funding and planning regulations being met. These include:

CARDIFF PARKWAY

This is a planned Parkway station to the east of Cardiff Central, being part of the Cardiff Hendre Lakes business development. It will be on the South Wales mainline south of the St Mellons Business Park and is hoped to be completed by 2023.

DEESIDE PARKWAY

This is a potential new Parkway station on the Wrexham to Bidston railway line in North East Wales. The Welsh Government selected this and three other potential stations in a 2019 report as being worthy of further detailed study.

DEVIZES PARKWAY

Plans for a Parkway station to serve to the Wiltshire town of Devizes (pop. 31,000) have been put forward by the Devizes Development Partnership. It would be sited on the A342 about three miles south of the town, on the London Paddington to Plymouth mainline.

FORT PARKWAY

This is a proposed Parkway station on the Birmingham to Tamworth line east of the city. Its name comes from the former Dunlop rubber factory called 'Fort Dunlop' situated near junction 5 of the M6 motorway. The site has been redeveloped as a hotel, offices and shopping complex but has no railway station nearby.

LEEDS-BRADFORD AIRPORT PARKWAY

The Harrogate Line Supporters Group have proposed a railway station for Leeds-Bradford Airport to be sited near Horsforth, north of Leeds on the Leeds to Harrogate line. Not only would it serve the airport but also the surrounding areas of Bramhope and Yeadon. It would be just one mile from the airport and an airport shuttle bus would connect the two sites.

NUNEATON PARKWAY

This is a proposed station on the Nuneaton to Hinckley stretch of line to the east of Nuneaton.

POLESWORTH PARKWAY

This would be on the West Coast mainline north of Rugby, situated close to the M42 and A5.

PORTWAY PARKWAY

This station in Bristol, which received planning permission in March 2019, will be built next to the Park and Ride facility of the same name, due for opening in 2021. The station is on the line from Bristol to Avonmouth and very near junction 18 of the M5, so it could get potential customers from the north and west of Bristol, as well as those who come over the Severn Bridge from South Wales. It is seen as part of the MetroWest scheme, which is designed to improve rail services in and around Bristol.

ROSEBERRY/NUNTHORPE PARKWAY

This proposed Parkway station would be between Nunthorpe and Great Ayton on the Esk Valley Line which runs between Middlesbrough and Whitby in the North East of England.

RUSHDEN PARKWAY

A proposed Parkway station for the Midland Main line would be built to the south east of Wellingborough by the A45 in Northamptonshire. It will serve the towns of Highham Ferrers and Rushden.

RUGBY PARKWAY

This is a proposed Parkway station on the West Coast Mainline to the south east of Rugby where the line to Northampton diverges, next to the A428 and near to junction 18 of the M1. It is hoped that the station will be open by 2026.

A view looking north of Ashchurch for Tewkesbury railway station which could be changed to Tewkesbury Parkway in the next few years. JOHN STRETTON

TEWKESBURY PARKWAY

This is not a new station, but rather a name change. The Ashchurch and Tewkesbury District Rail Promotion Group has put forward the case for changing the name of the existing station, 'Ashchurch for Tewkesbury' to 'Tewkesbury Parkway'. The station is on the Birmingham to Bristol mainline, six miles east of Tewkesbury.

THANET PARKWAY

A Parkway station in North East Kent has been proposed for the Canterbury to Ramsgate Line to the west of Ramsgate near to the A229 and the site of the former Manston Airport.

WEST WALES PARKWAY

This will be near to Felindre on the Swansea Avoiding Line which skirts round the northern fringes of Swansea. It is also near junction 46 of the M4 motorway and would be a railhead for passengers from the northern part of Swansea and other nearby communities.

CHAPTER 8

Other Parkway Stations

It is worthwhile briefly mentioning some other parkway stations found outside of Britain's railway system.

CALLERTON PARKWAY

This is a metro station stop on the Tyne & Wear Metro to the north west of Newcastle upon Tyne.

SWANLEY PARKWAY

This is in Swanley, Kent, on the Swanley New Barn Railway in Swanley Park, a 7½in (184mm) narrow gauge railway.

WEDNESBURY PARKWAY

This is situated on the West Midlands Metro train line which took over much of the old Great Western route between Birmingham Snow Hill and Wolverhampton low level. It is by the Wednesbury Park and Ride facility.

Outside of the UK in the Irish Republic there are two parkway railway stations, both in the greater Dublin area. The first is the unusually named 'M3 Parkway' situated right next to the M3 motorway in County Meath Ireland. It is the terminus station of the Docklands to M3 Parkway Western Commuter Service. The second is 'Navan Road Parkway' in Fingal on the Dublin to Sligo line near to Phoenix Park in west Dublin.

Postscript

Looking back over 50 years of Parkway stations, it could be argued that they have in the main been a success — some more than others. The rivalry between the car and the train that began in the 20th century meant railway planners had to look at new ways of bringing the motorist back onto the train. A Parkway railway station was just one way of doing that.

In the 21st century, with environmental concerns coming to the fore, government and council officials have looked at ways of reducing road traffic journeys and bringing people back to using public transport. Again, Parkway railway stations have been seen as one way of doing this. Plus, having a Park and Ride railway station on the edge of a town helps to reduce city centre congestion and pollution.

After all, Parkway railway stations are now seen as part of an integrated public transport system which can reduce car journeys and alleviate the stress of driving on the motorways to another town. In the words of the slogan, 'Let the train take the strain'.

Gallery

Chiltern Railways Class 165 *Networker* no 165029 waits to depart Aylesbury Vale Parkway on January 28, 2020.

A First Great Western HST train bound for Penzance has just departed from Bodmin Parkway station on April 4, 2013.

A Cross Country service for Newcastle waits at
Bristol Parkway station on July 14, 2019.

GBRf Class 66 no 66779 *Evening Star* in Brunswick Green livery waits
for a crew change at Coleshill Parkway station on February 2, 2019.

A Great Western Railway Class 800 *Intercity Express Train* speeds through Didcot Parkway with an express for London Paddington on July 14, 2019.

An East Midlands Trains Class 222 *Voyager* no 222021 leaving East Midlands Parkway on March 23, 2019, bound for Sheffield.

Chiltern Railways Class 165 *Networker* no 165019 departs Haddenham &
Thame Parkway with a service to London Marylebone on January 28, 2020.

A Northern Trains Class 156 *Super Sprinter* no 156463
arrives at Liverpool South Parkway with a service for
Liverpool Lime Street on November 10, 2018.

Chiltern Railways Class 168 *Clubman* No 168003 has just arrived at
Oxford Parkway with a service to Oxford on February 1, 2019.

A South Western Railway Class 444 *Desiro* no 444033
arrives at Southampton Airport Parkway with a
service to Weymouth on October 19, 2019.

A West Midlands Trains Class 172 *Turbostar* no 172336
departs from Stratford-upon-Avon Parkway on February
2, 2019 with a service for Stratford-upon-Avon.

A Greater Anglia Class 379 *Electrostar* no 379021 has just
arrived at Whittlesford Parkway from London Liverpool Street
with a service for Cambridge North on May 18, 2019.